With *Love* FROM A MOTHER'S HEART

Creating an Extraordinary Home

GLENDA REVELL

Foreword by
DONNA OTTO

BACK TO THE BIBLE®

WITH LOVE FROM A MOTHER'S HEART
published by Back to the Bible
1998 © by Glenda Revell

International Standard Book Number 0-8474-1103-6

Edited by Rachel Derowitsch
Cover design by Robert Greuter and Associates

For information:
BACK TO THE BIBLE
POST OFFICE BOX 82808
LINCOLN, NE 68501

1 2 3 4 5 6 7 8—04 03 02 01 00 99 98

Printed in the USA

In loving memory of Jean Culpepper Holland, whose extraordinary life of joyful self-sacrifice touched and changed forever the hearts of her husband, her children, her friends, her community and me.

The true calling of a Christian is not to do extraordinary things, but to do ordinary things in an extraordinary way.

—*Samuel Johnson*

Acknowledgments

A heart full of gratitude is owed and now lovingly given to the following:

My own dear spiritual mother, Elisabeth Elliot Gren, who, by her patient instruction and sacrificial love, has taught me more than could ever be contained in any book.

My beloved David (the love of my life), who has been a constant source of encouragement and support even as he ate innumerable "quick" meals so that I could cook up chapters.

My precious Charlotte, Sarah, Jason and Daniel, who were helpful, patient and quiet because "Mama's writing," and who are every day my inspiration and my joy.

My true spiritual daughter, Shannon Hardison, who aided me with her typing skills and inspired me with her beautifully transformed life.

My friend Dyan Wood, whose computer know-how saved the day and whose feedback and critiquing of the manuscript were invaluable to me.

My pastor, Tim Piland, whose teaching and exhortation from the Word of Truth enabled me, through a difficult time, to carry on and complete this task.

Those godly women who through the years have graciously taught me, by precept and example, how I ought to live, especially Lillian Hundley, Dot Sparks, Georgie Davey and Barbara Martin.

All of my friends at Gateway To Joy and Back to the Bible, especially:

Steve Nickel, who consistently and graciously gave godly counsel and encouragement.

Linda Meyers, whose enthusiasm and devoted friendship gave me strength.

Blaine Smith, who never ceased believing that this manuscript would materialize.

Rachel Derowitsch, my very capable editor, who understands her first calling and is faithful to it.

And all of my kind friends who permitted me to retell their memories and experiences.

To each and every one of you dear ones I would join my voice with that of the apostle Paul and say, "I thank my God every time I remember you. In all my prayers for all of you, I always pray with joy because of your partnership in the gospel from the first day until now, being confident of this, that he who began a good work in you will carry it on to completion until the day of Christ Jesus" (Phil. 1:3-6).

Contents

Foreword 11

Preface 13

1.   Our New Old House 19

2.   A Precious Cornerstone 25

3.   Our House Has *What*? .35

4.   Is There a Carpenter in the House? 65

5.   Help! Someone's Been Hurt! 79

6.   Somebody's at Your Door 93

7.   Poor, Pitiful Palace Dweller 105

8.   Peace and Contentment 119

9.   Peace and Order 131

10. Peace and Quiet 155

11. "He Can Stir His Own Coffee" 169

12. A Home Worth Remembering 189

13. Oh, Yes You Can! 205

Afterword 233

Notes 237

Foreword

Glenda Revell is an ordinary woman who, because she always said, "I'll try," has done extraordinary things.

With love from her heart, she gives a description for a Christian home and a prescription for your heart. No matter what your upbringing, you'll receive encouragement in her wit and wisdom as you fulfill your high and holy calling of being a wife and a mother.

She provides kind and gentle instruction based on the solid rock of Jesus and His Word. In each chapter you'll find a new frame of reference for meeting life's challenges.

Gently yet firmly, Glenda counsels you to make peace with God and others regardless of the cost. From her own experiences she knows the important difference between "keeping the peace" and "making the peace." If a difficult past is preventing you from establishing the kind of godly, orderly home you desire, her solid instruction and concrete suggestions will help you move beyond your pain. Glenda leads you through specific tasks that will refocus your attention and reshape your attitudes.

With refreshing transparency and vulnerability, warmth and truthfulness, Glenda addresses motherhood, marriage and managing self from the eternal perspective of Scripture and the common experiences of life. You will be blessed by her promise to pray for you and stimulated as she sends you out to "get your mess together."

It is my prayer that as you read *With Love From a Mother's Heart*, you will be influenced to create a home that will shape your family for many generations to come in the image of Christ.

Looking Up,
—*Donna Otto*
Author and Speaker
Scottsdale, Arizona

Preface

Several weeks ago I received a letter from a young mother that contained this poignant statement: "I stay at home and am trying to learn as much as I can about creating a Christian home. This is harder for me than graduate school since my past is so broken."

That same week I received a telephone call from an old acquaintance who tearfully exclaimed, "You have a perfect house and a perfect family and you won't tell me how you do it!" I was both crushed and amused by her frustration: crushed because I recognized my failure to take seriously the mandate given in Titus 2 to pass on to other women the lessons my Heavenly Father has taught me, and amused because I know how far from perfect my home and family are. Anything worthwhile that has ever been accomplished in our home or in our hearts is our Father's workmanship, for "unless the LORD builds the house, its builders labor in vain" (Ps. 127:1).

Even so, these and numerous other letters and conversations have tugged at me and convinced me of the tremendous need for older women to teach the younger. In previous generations, this concept was a given. Often three or more generations lived together under one roof, passing on child-rearing and home-making skills and helping to carry them out as well.

Today, the multigenerational, under-one-roof family has nearly disappeared. Grandma may be touring the nation in her RV or stashed away in a nursing home somewhere, removed from those who could benefit so greatly from her wealth of experience and wisdom.

Sometimes, younger women struggle alone because they are physically separated from their beloved mothers. Occasionally, emotional distance and bitterness cause the painful separation. Whatever the reason, it is difficult, sometimes terrifying, to be thrust into the role of wife and mother having no role model, no direction, no encouragement.

I know. I've been there. I would like to help.

To whom much is given, much is required (Luke 12:48). In the 23 years since I became a Christian, I have been given much: a loving, Christian husband, four delightful children, and a godly spiritual mother who has patiently, yet firmly, instructed me in righteousness. Now, it would seem, it is my turn to give back a portion of what I have received.

In studying God's Word, I see that I must also extend that motherly instruction to other "younger women" who are in need of encouragement and direction. The very thought of my "standing in the gap" for those who need help both humbles and excites me. I know what it has meant to me to have an older woman undertake for me. How thrilling it would be for me to do that for others! I also know my weaknesses and failures and wonder that God could ever call me to such an important task. But His Word is true and it is plain that I am called.

So, in this book I am offering what I can of myself to those who are hurting, those who are overwhelmed, those whose pasts are "broken."

My own children will tell you that if you are looking to be coddled, longing to be pampered and searching for the indulgent spiritual mother who will fulfill those desires, you've come to the wrong place. If, however, you yearn for someone who will tell you the truth, encourage you to be extraordinary and point you always to our only refuge, the cross of our Savior, Jesus Christ, then this very ordinary, fallible woman is at your service. I'll do the best I can to hold you to the highest standard, just as my spiritual mother always has done for me.

I want you to know, dear Daughter, that already I am very proud of you, for by just picking up this book you have demonstrated an openness to instruction and a desire to do well. As Charles Dickens said, "The will to do well is the next thing to having the power." Remember, your Heavenly Father is far more interested in your success than you are. Why would He not enable you to achieve it?

Following are the things I would tell you if I were your mother. Now, sit up straight and pay attention. I'm only going to say this once.

Electrical service can be installed; walls and porch decks can be rebuilt. But the foundation and underpinnings of a house are the strength and hope of the entire structure. If not solid and intact, there is no need to invest time and money in the decoration and function of the house. It will be for nothing.

1
Our New
Old House

March 3, 1990. Our oldest child's 12th birthday. Rainy. Gloomy. Cold. Little did we know how much our lives would change as a result of that day. Unsuspecting—that's what we were. And I'm glad.

The week before, an old friend had called—not so much in friendship as in her other role as real estate agent. "I saw a wonderful old house today that reminded me of you. You would love it! Would you like to see it?"

Her excitement was contagious, though I immediately took mental precautions against it. *We certainly aren't moving. Not a chance. And David decreed long ago that we would never own an old house "because you can't heat 'em." Besides, that house is thirty miles from David's job. He would never agree to commute that far when we have a perfectly adequate house just six miles from his work.*

I voiced the objections, trying to persuade myself as well as my friend.

"Oh, you don't have to buy it. I just thought you should see it, knowing how much you like old houses."

"Could I call you right back?" I asked.

David and I had a quick conference. "Sure, why don't you go?" he said. "You'll probably enjoy a trip into Smithfield with Frances. It's a quaint little town, right up your alley. Enjoy yourself."

It never crossed the outer edge of his imagination the danger he was in.

Two days later, Thursday, March 1, I came. I saw. I was conquered.

What it was about the 90-year-old ramshackle farmhouse that ensnared me on the spot I cannot say. True, it did have to its credit five charming fireplaces, ceilings with glorious height, unpainted, to-die-for woodwork, four porches and a few touches of gingerbread. But these could not possibly compensate for the badly cracked or caved-in walls, the rotted floors, the inadequate electrical service, the lack of a heating system, the one bathroom with no shower—well, you get the picture. In spite of all the commonsense reasons not to be, I was smitten. And so were the children.

That night at the dinner table there was much enthusiastic chatter about the old house on a country road in Smithfield. "You just *have* to see it," I pleaded with my husband. "I know we're not going to move there. It's an experience just to look at it."

"See if Frances has time to meet us there on Saturday," he consented, "and I'll go."

As dreary as that Saturday morning was, our spirits were cheerful as we left home for our "old-house adventure." The trip to Smithfield was uneventful, and when we got there I directed David to turn left onto Jericho Road. "And the walls came a-tumbling down." I smiled as I hummed the old spiritual. If only I had known how appropriate that song was.

"It's just over a little bridge, second house on the right," I told him. He pulled into the gravel driveway and, sure enough, Frances was already there waiting for us.

As we walked across the rickety back porch and entered the kitchen door we were hit with a dank, musty smell that didn't exactly say "Welcome Home." I immediately began to wonder what it was I had seen in the old place just two days earlier. *Must be the rain*, I thought. *Everything looks dismal in the rain.*

David endured the 45-minute tour as I pointed out "what could be done with this" and "what could be made of that." He had learned through the years that he could trust my vision for beautifying a house. And he was fascinated, more than he expected to be, by the grace and character of the antique domicile.

More fascinating to him, however, was the price. It was inexpensive, as houses go. In fact, downright cheap. "We could fix it up and have it paid for before I retire," he said.

David was beginning to show signs of real interest, just as I began to experience stomach-churning hesitation. *What have I done?* I wondered. *Is he really considering leaving our warm, comfortable home for this?* My dreadful suspicions were confirmed when he walked out to our old station wagon, pulled out the coveralls he had stashed away there, donned them and crawled under the miserable-looking structure. My husband, even while under the "old-house enchantment," was smart enough to know that the most important thing to consider when purchasing any house is the condition of the foundation. Electrical service can be installed; walls and porches can be rebuilt. But the foundation and underpinnings of a house are the strength and hope of the entire structure. If not solid and intact, there is no need to invest time and money in the decoration and function of the house. It will be for nothing.

Out crawled David about 20 minutes later, filthy but nodding and smiling. "She's as solid as can be," he said convincingly. So we talked. And prayed. And signed on the dotted line.

What on earth does getting into a mess like that have to do with establishing a Christian home? you may be wondering. Be patient. These things take time. Now get yourself a cup of tea and hurry back so I can tell you.

*T*herefore everyone who hears these words of mine and puts them into practice is like a wise man who built his house on the rock. The rain came down, the streams rose, and the winds blew and beat against the house; yet it did not fall because it had its foundation on the rock.

Matthew 7:24-25

2
A Precious
Cornerstone

Some would tell you that the underpinning of a Christian home is love—the sacrificial love of parents for each other and for their offspring and, yes, for God. Others would say it is religion or religious practices on which a home must be built.

Gracious! We might just as well expect paint and wallpaper to lend structural support! Don't you see? Those are only the lovely accouterments of a home. The foundation is something else indeed.

Long before the foundation of our house was built in 1902, the foundation of our Christian home (and yours) was firmly in place, comprised of the very stone the builders rejected—Christ Jesus Himself (Matt. 21:42). I didn't know it, though, and for many years I busily erected my life on nothing but shifting, sinking sand.

So how did I move from such a quagmire to a foundation of solid rock? I thought you'd never ask!

Reflecting over my childhood and youth, I realize that I was never anything but hungry—starving, really—for acceptance and love. Day in and day out I was occupied with the daunting task of finding anything that would make me acceptable to my family and to God. Do you know something of that fierce longing for love? Is it not painfully all-consuming?

My mother was an alcoholic. Now, don't let that trouble you on my behalf. I didn't know it then, but God makes no mistakes and I was never for a moment outside of His watch care. It really was impossible for me to please her, though, and being just a little girl, I was incapable of understanding that it was her sin rather than mine that made me unacceptable to her. I only understood that I craved her love and didn't have it. I convinced myself that if I somehow gave enough, tried hard enough and was good enough, she would eventually accept me and give me the tenderness for which my heart had yearned for so long. Unfortunately, an entire childhood spent in such effort resulted in abject failure. Why? Because my mother's requirements were unobtainable. It was hopeless.

Vivid are my memories of standing in the school yard during recess surrounded by the happy squeals and shouts of my classmates. I watched them run races, skip rope and scale the monkey bars, longing to join in the joyful ruckus.

I couldn't, however, because it was far too risky. I might dirty my dress or my white Mary Janes. A careful inspection awaited me when I returned home, and I knew I would be berated or beaten for any trace of "carelessness" or "foolishness." So I stayed to myself, leaning against the cold brick of the old schoolhouse, learning to taste fun through observation.

The sacrifice of my recesses, however, wasn't enough to make me acceptable to my mother. Somehow, a child's day affords far too many opportunities for scuffed shoes or a muddied dress or a thousand other mishaps. The standard was simply beyond my reach and I suffered for it.

Once, at the beginning of my fourth grade year, I managed to deposit a great blot of ink on the bodice of my brand-new school dress. I remember standing in the girl's room, tears streaming down my face, frantically scrubbing at the splotch with a soapy, soggy, brown paper towel. To this day I can smell that liquid soap, feel the cold water seeping through my undershirt, recall the paralyzing fear that gripped my heart as I watched, wild-eyed, in the mirror as the ugly stain lightened only slightly and spread. I was horrified at the prospect of standing before my drunken mother that afternoon in my ruined dress. But no matter how hard I tried, I couldn't clean myself up. Serious trouble awaited me that day and I knew it.

You may think it was very hard for me being raised under such demanding conditions. And so it was. But in looking back, I also see that it was a merciful thing. You see, God's mercy is always kind, but sometimes severe. George MacDonald expressed it this way:

> Thou worketh perfectly. And if it seem
> Some things are not so well, 'tis but because
> They are too loving deep, too lofty wise
> For me, poor child, to understand their laws.
> My highest wisdom, half is but a dream;
> My love runs helpless like a falling stream;
> Thy good embraces ill, and lo! its illness dies.[1]

Had I not spent years longing for the acceptance of my mother I might have been content as I was, never transferring that longing toward God. I would have experienced temporary satisfaction and eternal rejection.

It was the mercy of God that allowed the temporary rejection that I might obtain eternal acceptance. How much greater is that which I have been given than that which was withheld from me! His "good embraces ill and lo! its illness dies."

I eventually gave up all hope of ever pleasing my mother. Even the perpetual optimism of childhood had its limits. By the time I reached adolescence, I strove simply to survive in our home. My acceptance, I knew, was a lost cause.

Meanwhile, I had been attending church for a number of years, hoping to find God there, yearning to really know Him. I feared having to stand before Him someday, dirty and ashamed. Church attendance was one of the ways I hoped to "clean myself up." Surely, if I tried hard enough, I could gain His approval and His love. The trouble was, that awful stain on my life just kept spreading. So, I spent many years of squandered effort hoping to do the impossible and ended up, in my early 20s, as disillusioned and hopeless as I had been as a child standing in front of the sink, scrubbing away at my spoiled dress.

In spite of all my efforts, I was still dirty and unacceptable to God and I knew it, but I had no earthly idea of what to do about it. My resources were exhausted and so was I. I wanted to end my life.

It was then that God brought to me the wonderful message that changed everything. And it was the awful years of rejection that made me willing to receive that message—things "too loving deep, too lofty wise" for me to comprehend earlier.

Upon reading a Gospel tract, my eyes were opened to the truth that everyone is a sinner: "for all have sinned and fall short of the glory of God" (Rom. 3:23). I had no trouble believing I was a sinner. The stain of sin was my whole dirty problem.

I then saw that, throughout history, man has tried to rid himself of the problem through good works, religion, philosophy and morality—but without success. Once again I could easily relate.

My breath was taken away by the simplicity of the solution that was presented: God, being holy, could not lower His standard of righteousness. Being just, He had to punish sin. And being loving, He was not willing that any should perish. So He gave His only Son, Jesus Christ, the spotless Lamb of God, to suffer and die in my place, paying in full the penalty for my sin, so that I could be made clean. "You see, at just the right time, when we were still powerless, Christ died for the ungodly. . . . God demonstrates his own love for us in this: While we were yet sinners, Christ died for us" (Rom. 5:6, 8).

Even more mind-boggling was the truth that this acceptance and forgiveness are free gifts requiring no effort on my part. All I had to do was believe His Word and place my trust in the shed blood of Christ for my cleansing. "Yet to all who received him, to those who believed in his name, he gave the right to become children of God—children born not of natural descent, nor of human decision or a husband's will, but born of God" (John 1:12-13).

And that moment I believed.

At last, I was set free! "He lifted me out of the slimy pit, out of the mud and mire; he set my feet on a rock and gave me a firm place to stand" (Ps. 40:2). And best of all, I had been washed, adopted into God's family and, joy of all joys, accepted in the Beloved!

A former pastor of mine, the Reverend Donald B. Woodby, once gave a poignant illustration concerning that truth to our congregation. I recently called him and asked if he would kindly put it in writing for me. He graciously consented and his response follows:

Dear Glenda,

I was born and raised in central Michigan, where the winters are very cold. Temperatures of -20 degrees Fahrenheit are not uncommon. I remember times even colder than that.

My father was a schoolteacher and a farmer. We had a 160-acre farm and a flock of about 100 sheep. All of them were ewes except one or two bucks. We arranged the mating so the lambs would be born in January or February. This worked well for marketing the lambs late in the fall.

When the lambs began to arrive we kept the sheep in the lower level of the barn. When we saw that a lamb was about to be born, we put the mother sheep in a small pen. During this lambing season, my father and I would take turns going out to the barn about every two hours to see that everything was going all right.

Sometimes a lamb died. Other times a mother sheep died and left a lamb with no mother. It happened almost every year. One might think the obvious answer to such a problem would be to take the living lamb with no mother and place it in a pen with a mother whose lamb had died. This could be a solution except for one major problem: the mother sheep knew her lamb by smell. She would not accept the orphan lamb. If the lamb was put in a pen with the mother who had lost her lamb, she would butt it away. Soon the lamb would die.

What was the solution? It was quite simple. We would take a sharp knife and skin the lamb that had died. Then, we would take a strong string and tie the skin on the lamb that had been rejected. The mother would then smell the lamb and, because the smell was that of her own lamb, permit the living lamb to nurse and claim the nursing lamb as her very own. In a moment there was a bonding between a sheep that had lost her lamb and a lamb that had lost its mother. A motherless lamb was accepted by the death of another.

The Bible states that "Christ died for our sins" (1 Cor. 15:3). Ephesians 1:6 says that God "hath made us accepted in the Beloved" (i.e., Christ, KJV). Also, Romans 13:14—"But put ye on the Lord Jesus Christ" (KJV)—shows that personal salvation results when a sinner has received Jesus Christ as Lord and there is a blessed union between Christ and a repentant sinner. "Christ in you the hope of glory" is the message of Colossians 1:27 (KJV).

As a boy and then a young man I had no understanding of this. If I had been asked how a person gets to heaven, I would have stated, "Do the best you can, follow the Ten Commandments, go to church, follow the Golden Rule, live a life of good works, and no doubt God will accept you." But as you know, Glenda, this is not the way it is. Just as you heard the Gospel of our Lord and received it with joy, I, too, heard the message of salvation by faith and not by works.

That was nearly fifty years ago. Jesus and His death on the cross for my sin is still blessed to my heart. Soon after my conversion, I remembered the experience my father and I had in saving the life of a motherless lamb. It was made possible by the death of another. I thank God that He has accepted me because of the death of Jesus Christ.

Sincerely,

Pastor Woodby

My dear Child, are you longing with all of your heart for acceptance and love? Have you, by the mercy of God, experienced the pain of temporary rejection that you might seek the eternal benefit of a life hidden in Christ? May I point you now to my blessed Savior, whose arms are open wide for you, who will never leave you, who, when all others have forsaken you, will take you up? Will you receive Him now, trusting Christ alone as your Savior and Lord?

"So this is what the Sovereign LORD says: 'See, I lay a stone in Zion, a tested stone, a precious cornerstone for a sure foundation; the one who trusts will never be dismayed'" (Isa. 28:16).

"For no one can lay any foundation other than the one already laid, which is Jesus Christ" (1 Cor. 3:11).

Brothers, I do not consider myself yet to have taken hold of it. But one thing I do: Forgetting what is behind and straining toward what is ahead, I press on toward the goal to win the prize for which God has called me heavenward in Christ Jesus.

Philippians 3:13-14

3
Our House
Has What?

About a year after we purchased our 90-plus-year-old house, we discovered that we got more in the bargain than a charming fixer-upper on a firm foundation. We expected all along that restoring the place would be neither easy nor cheap. By the end of that first year, experience had confirmed our expectations. We were exhausted and penniless. Our "to do" list was still a mile long. And that wasn't all.

I began noticing a white powdery substance here and there on the pine floors. Not all of the time, not everywhere, but occasionally, in certain spots. Then a little more often in a few more places. Under different circumstances we might have been more troubled by this mysterious occurrence, but our days (and nights) were filled with rewiring, replumbing, plastering, painting, wallpapering, stenciling, laying carpet and adding light fixtures, receptacles, appliances and a heating system. At the same time, we were caring for our four children, and my husband still found 40 hours of spare time each week for his "other" job. So, tiny hills of white powder seemed a trifle. We were busy attending to the important matters.

As weeks and months passed, the powder piles became harder and harder to ignore. One day while talking to another old-house owner, I mentioned the problem and he immediately told me what he thought it might be. I told David about it that night,

t day he called a pest-control company. Sure
'iagnosis was confirmed. The powder was extra-
___st. The entire time we had been killing ourselves to
improve the livability and appearance of our house, a silent, unseen enemy was undermining it all—powder post beetles. They
were legion and they were ours.

The solution was simple—call the exterminator—but not
easy—*pay* the exterminator. We were fortunate, though, to have
caught the problem before more extensive damage was done.
So we paid the price gladly, rather than risk losing everything
for which we had worked so hard and so long.

Later, we talked about how foolish we had been to think we
were attending to matters of importance and ignoring trifles
when it was actually the other way around. Think of it. Tiny insects that we couldn't even see were weakening the entire structure of the house we thought we were restoring.

That precisely illustrates the reason why I cannot, in good
conscience, as one who cares and prays for you, permit you to
dash headlong into the tangibles of "keeping house" while dis-
regarding the hidden forces that would unravel your dreams for
a peaceful home. These destroyers are powerful and pervasive,
and worst of all, they are frequently unperceived until irreme-
diable damage is done.

If that isn't frightening enough, we wives and mothers are
often the ones who unwittingly unleash these enemies on our
homes and families day after day. Powder post beetles are nothing compared to the voracious pests I'm about to describe. Bitterness, anger, resentment and self-pity—that rowdy pack of
troublemakers that have been stowaways in our hearts since the
time when we were so wounded and injured by someone we
loved—are the forces with which we must reckon. Not tomorrow. Not after reading the rest of the book. Now, before it's too
late.

Once again the solution is simple but not easy. Simple, because those of us who are accepted in the Beloved have the
strength to disperse these enemies into disorderly flight. We
have power. We are more than conquerors (Rom. 8:37).

Why, then, are so many of us unsuccessful in battle? Because it isn't easy. It costs a great deal. We must be willing to let go of our pasts and our tendency to excuse ourselves from responsibility because of them. This will entail taking on an entirely changed point of view and developing a new pattern of thinking. Sounds heavy, doesn't it? Well, it is. Heavy and requisite.

You see, like powder post beetles, bitterness and his gang of angry relatives never just leave on their own. They stay and gnaw and munch and chew. You might not even know they are there, but soon other people know—especially the ones you love the most. Your fuse is short. You often find yourself immersed in angry remembrances of those who have hurt you. You mentally fondle each painful incident, every stinging word. Bitterness, resentment and self-pity form the three-stranded cord that tightly binds you to your past. You're not even sure you *want* to be free. Bondage is at least familiar. What choice do you have, anyway?

Oh, if only I could give your shoulders a loving shake and look you directly in the eye as I tell you this! You *can* be free. You *do* have a choice. *Choice* is the operative word here. I will be using it often. But for now, let's listen to someone else who made a choice concerning his past: "Brothers, I do not consider myself yet to have taken hold of it. But one thing I do: Forgetting what is behind and straining toward what is ahead, I press on toward the goal to win the prize for which God has called me heavenward in Christ Jesus" (Phil. 3:13-14).

Does that not spark even the tiniest interest in you? Don't you really want to leave your past behind you, striving to be the best you can possibly be for God and for your family? True, it will cost you. But what you will receive in return will be exceedingly, abundantly above all you could ask or think. God, who cannot lie, promises you that.

What differentiates a wise from a foolish woman? "The wise woman builds her house, but with her own hands the foolish one tears her down" (Prov. 14:1). Certainly we can observe the differences in their behavior, but the primary difference is in their thinking. A foolish woman is one whose thinking is conformed to this world. She has been trained to have it her way, look out for number one, do it if it feels good, don't do it if it doesn't and defend her personal rights at any cost. She believes that her me-first attitude is her ticket to freedom, while in reality it forges the chains of her captivity. Paul warned about such thinking nearly 2,000 years ago: "See to it that no one takes you captive through hollow and deceptive philosophy, which depends on human tradition and the basic principles of this world rather than on Christ" (Col. 2:8).

The inevitable result of adhering to such deceptive philosophy is disappointment. No one has it her own way all of the time or even most of the time. Suffering is universal to those inhabiting this fallen, sinful world. As a former pastor of mine once said, "If you aren't presently suffering, and if you haven't recently suffered, don't look now but the dump truck's a-comin'." Such repeated disappointment opens the gate to the seduction of self-pity: Why did God let my loved one die? Why couldn't I have had a normal childhood? Why is my husband so hard to get along with? Why can't I ever please him? How could my children be so ungrateful after all I've done for them? Why won't God allow me to become pregnant? Why did God allow me to become pregnant? Why can't I have a fulfilling job? And on and on and on. Before long this disillusioned, hurting and angry woman is, with her own hands, tearing her house down.

A woman who is wise, on the other hand, has the same natural desires and expectations as the foolish woman, but has followed Paul's admonition to the Romans (12:1-12). Having offered her body, thoughts, desires and attitudes as a sacrifice to God, she does not conform herself to the pattern of this world but is transformed by the renewing of her mind. Only then, says Paul, will she be able to discern the will of God. Paradoxically, this act of submitting all to God, which to the world looks like bondage, results in absolute freedom, contentment and peace.

So, where do we begin the process of having our minds renewed and transformed? At Calvary, of course, where everything is made new. Here we see displayed for time and eternity the mind of Jesus, even as we gaze upon Him, writhing in agony and shame. "Your attitude should be the same as that of Christ Jesus: who, being in very nature God, did not consider equality with God something to be grasped, but made himself nothing, taking the very nature of a servant, being made in human likeness. And being found in appearance as a man, he humbled himself and became obedient unto death—even death on a cross!" (Phil. 2:5-8).

There is no looking out for number one here, only a laying down of all rights even unto the most hideous, torturous form of death devised by man. Jesus, who was God, overcame the world by obedient submission. We overcome the world and our pasts of sin and pain exactly the same way. When we become obedient to death—death to self—God is free to gloriously transform our thinking. Then we can live victoriously, as we are commanded in Romans 12:21: "Do not be overcome by evil, but overcome evil with good."

Does this sound lovely but implausible? Would I better understand the impossibility of it if only I could hear your particular case? Let me assure you that God is a loving Father who never asks more from His children than they can give. He does not command us to overcome evil with good and then desert us to the task. He tenderly, lovingly leads us every step of the way, supplying His strength when we are weak, His guidance when we have lost our way, His Spirit when we need comfort, His forgiveness when we fail. I know this to be true because He has lifted me out of a broken past, "out of the miry clay," as the psalmist wrote, and "set my feet upon a Rock, and established my goings" (Ps. 40:2, KJV).

May I entreat you now to stay with me as I reveal a few of the lessons I learned at the feet of my Heavenly Father during my 23 years as His child? This, of course, is not an exhaustive list, nor is it given as the last word on "overcoming evil with good."

Neither is it supplied here as a simplistic solution or denial of your brokenness and pain. Rather, it is a record of truths about God and about myself, the understanding of which released me from captivity to self and to the world's hollow and deceptive philosophy. I set them forth for you now prayerfully and as tenderly as I know how.

The Sovereignty of God

First and above all, I had to learn to trust in the sovereignty of God. He is perfectly holy, perfectly loving and perfectly sovereign. (If you hold arguments against any or all of these three premises, I recommend C. S. Lewis's *The Problem of Pain* and Elisabeth Elliot's *A Path Through Suffering*. These two books are enormously enlightening to anyone who believes a loving God, if truly sovereign, would prevent suffering.) Nothing is out of His control even when everything appears to be. The One whose infinite wisdom hurled everything that is into existence knows exactly what will prove to be for my ultimate good. "'For I know the plans I have for you' declares the LORD, 'plans to prosper you and not to harm you, plans to give you hope and a future'" (Jer. 29:11).

God knows the plans He has for us. We do not know. He deals with us and brings about His plans for us within the context of a sin-cursed world, using sinful people—the only kind there are. Our circumstances may appear to be brought about by the neglect or ill will of those who hate us or wish evil upon us, but He is steadily working behind the scenes to turn those circumstances into prosperity, hope and a future. The trouble is, we can't see behind the scenes. That's what faith is for.

E. B. Pusey wrote,

This, then, is of faith, that everything, the very least, or what seems to us great, every change of the seasons, everything which touches us in mind, body, or estate, whether brought about through this outward senseless nature, or by the will of man, whether good or bad, is overruled to each of us by the all-holy, all-loving will of God. Whatever befalls us, however it befalls us, we must receive as the will of

God. If it befalls us through man's negligence, or anger, still it is, to us the will of God. For if the] could happen to us without God's permission, it ..._ something out of God's control. God's providence or His love would not be what they are. Almighty God Himself would not be the same God: not the God whom we believe, adore, and love.

Everything that happens to us is overruled by the will of our loving God. What peace is to be gained from believing this awesome fact! My life was changed by it as I ceased to think of my lost childhood as some tragic accident and understood it as the will of God for me. Acceptance replaced the root of bitterness in my heart, and, as Amy Carmichael wrote, "in acceptance lieth peace." David wrote, "LORD, you have assigned me my portion and my cup; you have made my lot secure" (Ps. 16:5). What security there is for me in understanding that my portion and my cup—meaning all that touches me—are chosen for me by God.

In *Morning Watches/Night Watches*, a devotional book written in 1883 by John R. Macduff, I came upon this succinct yet powerful statement concerning the sovereignty of God: "How it would keep the mind from its guilty proneness to brood and fret over second causes, were this grand but simple truth ever realized—that all that befalls us are integral parts in a stupendous plan of wisdom—that there is no crossing or thwarting the designs and dealings of God; none can say 'what doest Thou?'— All ought to say, 'He doeth all things well.'"

My past, present and future circumstances are integral parts in a stupendous plan of wisdom! Can you join in the joyous affirmation, "He doeth all things well"? Will you, with the faith of a little child, lift your face into the light of His countenance and say with the psalmist, "Lord, you have assigned me my portion and my cup"? Then can you repeat the words of the One who died for you: "Shall I not drink the cup the Father has given me?"

> All is of God that is, and is to be,
> And God is good. Let this suffice us still,

Resting in childlike trust upon His will,
Who moves to His great ends, unthwarted by the ill.
— J. G. Whittier

Eternal Perspective

The Word of God describes this life as a "mist that appears for a little while and then vanishes" (James 4:14). Life is momentary. What fraction of that moment consists of suffering?

When attempting to explain this important principle to my children, I draw on our eight-foot-long chalkboard an unbroken line from one end to the other. I explain to them that the line represents all of eternity, so they must imagine that it doesn't end where the chalkboard ends but continues in both directions for ever and ever. Then I place somewhere on the line a tiny dot, which represents the span of one lifetime. (Keep in mind the difficulty of drawing eternity to scale!) "Suppose this is your life," I tell them. "Now suppose it is your lot to suffer for the duration of your life. In view of eternity, what difference will it make? What does it matter what is taken from you or what you give up, what is done to you or what hardship you endure?"

Of course it would matter to you now. It would matter a great deal. But remember, I said "in view of eternity." When you imagine how infinitesimal even the longest possible life would appear on an eternal line, your perspective changes. Self-pity suffers the deprivation of her footing. All that awaits gains preeminence over what is.

The apostle Paul said it this way: "I consider that our present sufferings are not worth comparing with the glory that will be revealed in us" (Rom. 8:18). "Therefore we do not lose heart. Though outwardly we are wasting away, yet inwardly we are being renewed day by day. For our light and momentary troubles are achieving for us an eternal glory that far outweighs them all" (2 Cor. 4:16-17).

Everything we endure—every pang, every loss, every sorrow—is temporary. Oh, but the love of God, the salvation of our souls, the glory that shall be revealed—these are everlasting.

Don't miss the repeated correlation in Scripture between

today's suffering and tomorrow's glory. Not only do they appear together in passages throughout the writings of Paul (and as the theme of 1 Peter), but he even states in the above passage from 2 Corinthians 4 that it is our suffering that achieves eternal glory for us. Why? I am neither learned nor intelligent enough to conduct such a study. I am aware, however, of two of God's doubtless myriad purposes in linking our suffering to future glory, and they both contain mystery. We find one in Hebrews 5, where the writer, speaking of our Savior, said, "Although he was a son, he learned obedience from what he suffered" (v. 8). Why the spotless Son of God needed to learn obedience I cannot fathom. Why I need to learn obedience I know quite well. Then, in 1 Peter 4 we are given the astonishing information that when we suffer we are actually participating in Christ's sufferings! "Dear friends, do not be surprised at the painful trial you are suffering, as though something strange were happening to you. But rejoice that you participate in the sufferings of Christ, so that you may be overjoyed when his glory is revealed" (vv. 12-13). Why do we share in His sufferings? Romans 8:17 says it is so we may also share in His glory! Is it any wonder Paul said our present sufferings aren't worth comparing to the glory that shall be revealed in us? We will someday exchange momentary troubles for eternal glory. What a deal!

Francis de Sales, who lived from 1567 to 1622, wrote, "You must form clearly in yourself the idea of eternity. Whoever thinks well on this troubles himself little about what happens in these three or four moments of mortal life." [1]

Three or four *moments* of mortal life. Let that concept sink in. Do you feel the grip of your sorrow loosening? Can you bear your loss or your illness or your emotional pain valiantly when you consider that it is momentary? Why not stop right now and ask your eternal Father to effect such a change in your perspective today. You have nothing to lose but misery.

Focus

Let's face it. Most of us spend an enormous amount of time thinking about ourselves, our needs and our circumstances.

be more important to me than I? Unfortunately, [o]ur[?] [nat]ural tendency lends itself to despondency and de[?] [?] why God has given us clear instruction that we are to focus our attention elsewhere. "Let us fix our eyes upon Jesus, the author and perfecter of our faith, who for the joy set before him endured the cross, scorning the shame, and sat down at the right hand of the throne of God" (Heb. 12:2). The Greek word *aphorao*, which means "to direct our gaze on God and to turn it away from everything else," is used in this text. The writer goes on to say, "Consider him who endured such opposition from sinful men, so that you will not grow weary and lose heart" (v. 3). So by changing our focus from self, circumstances and all else to heaven and Christ, we prevent discouragement in ourselves and weariness in our duties.

In Colossians 3:1-2, Paul expresses it this way: "Since, then, you have been raised with Christ, set your hearts on things above, where Christ is seated at the right hand of God. Set your minds on things above, not on earthly things." You may spend thousands of dollars on therapy and never receive counsel as helpful as this admonition of your wise Father. He is, after all, the One named Wonderful Counselor.

God understands the intricacies of our psyches. He knows that the more we look inward, examine our pain and make it our focal point, the more disconsolate we become. Before long, our difficulties have taken on mammoth proportions and we are overwhelmed by the grotesque sight of our "victimhood."

It doesn't have to be that way. We can choose (there's that word again) to focus our attention on the One in whom we are hidden. While concentrating on Christ—His holiness, His suffering, His great love for us—the horrors of our own trials begin to pale.

On her radio program *Gateway To Joy*, Elisabeth Elliot stated the case this way:

> Keep looking toward heaven.
> Look around and you'll be dismayed.
> Look inside and you'll be depressed.
> Look up and you'll be thrilled!

Keep in mind that we are not talking about repression or denial here. Those are defense mechanisms of which the Christian has no need. We have a Savior who drank unflinchingly from the cup of suffering His Father had prepared for Him. How could He do it? His heart and mind were not focused on His unfathomable suffering but on doing the will of His Father.

As always, we would do well to follow His example. It is our duty to endure the cross without focusing on it, turning our thoughts to the joy that is set before us.

Theodore Monod wrote,

Looking unto Jesus as long as we remain on the earth. We must look unto Jesus from moment to moment, without allowing ourselves to be distracted by memories of a past which we should leave behind us nor by an occupation with a future of which we know nothing.

Looking unto Jesus always with a gaze more and more constant, more and more confident, "changed into the same image from glory to glory" (2 Cor. 3:18). Thus, we await the hour when He will call us to pass from earth to heaven and from time to eternity, the promised hour, the blessed hour, when at last "we shall be like Him; for we shall see Him as He is" (1 John 3:2).[2]

The time is near when we shall be like the One on whom our gaze is fixed. Why waste precious days and hours focused on the depressing circumstances of our pilgrimage when we could be advantageously occupied with the glory of His face?

O soul are you weary and troubled,
No light in the darkness you see?
There's light for a look at the Savior,
And life more abundant and free.

Turn your eyes upon Jesus,
Look full in His wonderful face,
And the things of earth will grow strangely dim,
In the light of His glory and grace.
— Helen H. Lemmel

Emotion vs. the Will

While it would be unwise to deny our feelings (God knows what they are anyway), it is infinitely more foolish to base our decisions on them, particularly in matters as important as obedience to God. Emotions vacillate. They are affected by circumstances, hormones, illness and the weather. As children of God, we are held accountable to Him for obedience to His Word whether or not we "feel like it." It is not by our emotions but by our will that we must act.

Nowhere does God command us to *be* or *feel* thankful or forgiving or charitable or loving. He simply commands us to give thanks, to forgive, to show kindness and to love one another. That is why it is not hypocritical, contrary to the world's thinking, to obey God even when our emotions are screaming in protest. God is concerned with our will. That is who we are. If we will to obey Him in contradiction of our uncontrollable feelings, and then we obey Him, more often than not our feelings will follow.

This principle is clearly explained in Hannah Whitall Smith's *The Christian's Secret of a Happy Life*. In a chapter entitled "Difficulties Concerning the Will," she states: "Cease to consider your emotions, for they are the servants; and regard simply your will which is the real king in your being. Is that given up to God? Is that put into His hands? Does your will decide to believe? Does your will choose to obey? If this is the case, then *you* are in the Lord's hands, and *you* decide to believe, and *you* choose to obey; for your will is yourself. And the thing is done. The transaction with God is as real, when only your will acts, as when every emotion coincides. It does not seem as real to you; but in God's sight it is as real."[3]

So, you see, you may at any time decide in your will to abandon yourself to some act of obedience to God, confessing to Him simultaneously that you feel like doing nothing of the sort; and still He receives the act as obedience.

For the purpose of illustration, let's say your next-door neighbor and good friend (you thought) says something shockingly malicious about you. It is clear from her statements and behavior towards you that you have been grossly misunderstood. The only thing you know to do is to go to her and make an attempt to clear up the mistake, but she rudely refuses to hear you. She shuts you out. Your friend has become an enemy.

As soon as you recover from disbelief, all sorts of emotions flood over you. You're wounded and angry. You feel rejected, isolated, resentful. The more you think about it, the more indignant you become. "Of all the nerve!" you fume.

The next morning you read your Bible, as is, of course, your custom, and your reading takes you to Luke 6:27-28: "But I tell you who hear me: Love your enemies, do good to those who hate you, bless those who curse you, pray for those who mistreat you." Your emotions rise up in wild protest. "NO! NO! NO! Please not that! ANYTHING but that!" they shriek.

At that moment you make a choice: you put into effect the strong will your mother always accused you of having, or you allow your clamoring emotions to rule. So, which will it be?

Anyone who is acquainted with you knows with certainty that you will do the right thing, so let's look in on the scene as it unfolds.

Your head is bowed and you cry out to God for help. Then you unload all of your anguish and anger on Him because He cares for you. Tears flow. Your face begins to soften. "Help me to love her," you whisper. "Show me ways to be good to her. Bless her, O my God, and her family with good things. In the name of Christ my Lord, Amen."

What has just happened, my Friend, is obedience, pure and simple. You may by now feel more loving toward your neighbor, or you may not. But remember, God never told you to feel anything—only to submit your will to His. Then He enabled you to do it. You can be sure that He will work in your heart to restore love and will provide, if you are alert, opportunity to do good to your neighbor. Then you again must choose God's will against your feelings (if they haven't yet rallied around), and on it goes.

Before leaving the subject of will versus emotion, let's move from the hypothetical to the appalling truth. Life for most of us contains trials far more devastating than putting up with a gossipy neighbor. "Fiery" trials, Peter aptly named them (1 Pet. 4:12, NKJV). Are we held as strictly accountable for obedience in the midst of these as in lesser trials? You know the answer, don't you? Obedience doesn't become optional simply because circumstances become painful. God is the same yesterday, today and forever, and so are His commands.

Our Savior's obedience even unto death is our supreme example. What trial do we face that compares to His? Yet we read nothing about how He felt while being mocked and stripped and beaten—only that He endured. Jesus faced rejection that we will never experience. The Father, who has promised He will never leave us, in that black hour on Calvary turned His back on our precious Savior. Yet Christ never opened His mouth in complaint. Did He not have feelings? "For we do not have a high priest who is unable to sympathize with our weaknesses, but we have one who has been tempted in every way, just as we are—yet was without sin" (Heb. 4:15). Of course Jesus had feelings. He suffered in every way just as we suffer. I suspect the intensity of His emotional suffering far exceeded anything we could experience due to the refined sensibilities of His holy nature. But He laid aside His feelings, and it is His obedience, not His feelings, that are recorded for us in Scripture.

There are other examples in the Bible of men and women who were stretched beyond anything we could imagine, who understood the will of God and did it even in the most severe circumstances. Hebrews 11 gives example after example of those who chose to follow God notwithstanding intense suffering. There is no record given, however, of how they felt about the messes they were in. Let's look at one of these, my favorite.

"By faith Moses, when he had grown up, refused to be known as the son of Pharaoh's daughter. He chose to be mistreated along with the people of God rather than to enjoy the pleasures of sin for a short time. He regarded disgrace for the sake of

Christ as of greater value than the treasures of Egypt, because he was looking ahead to his reward" (Heb. 11:24-26).

Those three sentences show us the will of Moses. Refusing and choosing are acts of the will. They also show us an abdication of his feelings: rather than enjoy the pleasure of sin he chose to suffer. And, in case you didn't notice, a healthy dose of eternal perspective and heavenly focus is included: he was looking ahead for his reward. Did he spend lonely nights pacing the floor in anguished indecision? Was he terrified of the brutality he would suffer at the hands of the Egyptians? Did he weep and mourn for the parents who had given him up for adoption? We aren't told. God only reveals what he *did*.

The same could be said concerning the other men and women of faith whose lives are made an open book for us in the 11th chapter of Hebrews. They were flesh and blood and bone and sinew. They felt pain and heartache, anguish and fear. They were only human, just like us. But they were placed in God's biblical hall of fame for our example and encouragement because they demonstrated strength of will. They obeyed God in the face of overwhelming adversity. And if you doubt for a moment that they experienced the same emotions that wreak havoc in our hearts today, read what God says about them and promises to them: "They were longing for a better country—a heavenly one. Therefore God is not ashamed to be called their God, for he has prepared a city for them" (v. 16).

And what will He do for them in that Holy City? "He will wipe every tear from their eyes. There will be no more death or mourning or crying or pain, for the old order of things will be passed away" (Rev. 21:4).

Can you subordinate your emotions to your will for this fleeting moment of difficulty, knowing that God Himself will wipe away every tear from your eyes? Will you walk in obedience to God with such resolve that He will say of you what was written of those believers of old, "The world was not worthy of them" (Heb. 11:38)? Of course you can, and you will, for the One who calls you is faithful and He will do it.

Control of Thought Life

Those who investigate human brain processes tell us that grooves or tracks are formed from infancy as we develop our own unique patterns of thinking. As we mature, we continuously add cars to our train of thought, but the train still follows the established track. For most people, this process is simply one piece in the complicated puzzle of their personality. It helps make them who they are. For others, however, it may lead to catastrophe when the track is laid, for chemical, biological or environmental reasons, along a destructive path. While there have been tremendous advances, especially in chemical intervention of some psychological disorders, honest practitioners of psychotherapy admit that they are unable to offer any consistently successful solutions for most thought trains run amuck.

Not so with God. His therapy was prescribed long before scientists recognized the existence of this enigma. "The weapons we fight with are not the weapons of this world. On the contrary, they have divine power to demolish strongholds. We demolish arguments and every pretension that sets itself up against the knowledge of God, and we take captive every thought to make it obedient to Christ" (2 Cor. 10:4-5).

God's children have—not *will* have at some future time, or *may* have if circumstances are favorable, but *now* have—divine power to demolish strongholds (established patterns of thinking). The power is in the weapons God gives us. Weaponry implies warfare, and war is (rephrased for the fainthearted) the antithesis of heaven. This explains why so many Christians live in defeat rather than derailing their errant thought patterns. They'd like to have victory, of course, but preparing for battle is strenuous work and the actual fight is murderous. Who would volunteer for such a struggle?

Like Uncle Sam on the U.S. Army posters, God points His finger at you and me. He wants us armed. He wants us to know our enemy. He wants us in the fray.

Furthermore, God offers His soldiers something Uncle Sam never could—a promised victory through divine power. But He never promised it would be easy.

The greatest difficulty is in learning to recognize the enemy at work. Satan is a crafty foe, and you can be sure he's taken great pains to ascertain the exact position of your vulnerabilities. His weapons are the flaming arrows of fallacious thoughts, hurled into us with calculated accuracy. He waits for an opportune moment—often a time of fatigue, illness or some other form of severe stress—then, *zing*, the assault ensues from every direction. Before you're aware of what's happening, your train of thought is racing down the track, bringing you along for a dreadfully bumpy and dangerous ride.

Since I've never experienced your pattern of thinking, I cannot know the route it takes. Your genetic makeup and your life experiences (which are yours alone) make it what it is. The same is true for mine. But I suspect that the enemy's tactics in using those thought patterns for his nasty purposes are astonishingly similar for both of us. For that reason, I will give you a peek at a thought pattern to which I am prone and then show you how God enabled me to take those thoughts captive, bringing them to obedience in Christ.

No one really cares for me, might be the initial arrow of the sneak attack. (It must be noted that I probably couldn't have prevented that first hit. The Christian life is spiritual warfare; enemy fire is expected. What I choose to do at this point, however, is my responsibility. I have divine weapons, but I don't have to use them. Surrender seems much easier than standing firm; parlaying with the enemy much more agreeable than resisting him.) *Of course no one cares for me*, the attack proceeds. *My own mother didn't even want me. Why should I expect anyone else to? I can't do anything right. . . . I'm completely worthless to God and to everyone else. . . . I might just as well give up. . . . Anybody could do what I do better than I do it. . . . I'm always going to be lonely and miserable and nobody even cares.* Well, I'm sure you get the picture. Ugly, isn't it? It's obvious what such continued thinking would accomplish. It breeds self-absorption, self-pity, bitterness and resentment. It keeps our focus and perspective on the temporal and undermines our trust in a sovereign God. So, how do we deflect the fiery darts from the outset?

First, *be alert*. Our enemy is a roaring lion, seeking whom he may devour (1 Pet. 5:8). He stages his attacks during our weakest moments. If we fail to eat properly, take reasonable care of our bodies and get enough rest, we become sitting ducks for demonic target practice. This seems so obvious as to not bear mentioning, but many Christians neglect this important part of their basic training. Yes, the warfare is spiritual, but our existence is physical. The two are inextricably entwined.

Second, *pray*. "Lord, save me!" was the effective cry of Peter as he attempted to walk on the water to Jesus (Matt. 14:29). At the first whisper of a negative thought, a heart raised in supplication to God can stop the process before it starts. "My Father, I am assailed by arguments and pretenses that set themselves up against the knowledge of Christ in me. Deliver me from this evil, now, I pray in the name of my Lord and Savior, Jesus Christ."

"God is our refuge and strength, an ever-present help in trouble" (Ps. 46:1). What good is refuge not taken? "Call to me and I will answer you and show you great and unsearchable things you do not know" (Jer. 33:3). But you must call.

Third, *use Scripture*. When Jesus was tempted in the wilderness He quoted Scripture. We can effectively rout the enemy using the same method. You've had a glimpse into one of my downward-spiraling thought patterns. Verses that have been useful to me include any that assure me of God's love for and faithful care of me. Jeremiah 31:3 is one example: "I have loved you with an everlasting love; I have drawn you with lovingkindness." The more of these verses I commit to memory, the larger my stockpile of munitions.

You know the area in which you are weakest concerning your thought life. Find verses of Scripture that counter those strongholds, and then memorize them and use them at the first sign of attack. Don't wait until you've indulged in self-pity. You must strike early and forcefully if you're to have victory. And remember, any suggestion of Satan's is a lie. God's Word is truth. The truth shall set you free (John 8:32).

Fourth, *sing*. The psalmist spoke of being surrounded with songs of deliverance (Ps. 32:7). Learn some hymns and songs of praise and have them ready for the onslaught. I've found a few rousing verses of "A Mighty Fortress Is Our God" sends the tempter fleeing. Whether it's the powerful words or the sound of my voice that does the trick, I really can't say. Either way, we wouldn't want to knock success. A different hymn might prove more effective for you. Just be discriminating. "Nobody Knows the Trouble I've Seen" would be a poor choice under the circumstances. Look for words that glorify God and describe our dependence on His protective power over us.

Fifth, *eat spiritual food*. It amazes me how much consideration some Christians give to what they feed their bodies while giving no thought to their spiritual diets. Don't be misled about the importance of what we feed our minds. No one can prepare for spiritual warfare while squandering huge blocks of time reading romance novels and magazines or watching soap operas and talk shows. Get yourself into training by making a practice of reading a portion of the Bible every day. If you have time for more reading, try some biographies of great Christians such as Amy Carmichael, Elizabeth Prentiss and Susannah Wesley. Saturate your mind with God's point of view. Spend time with other Christians and, most of all, spend time with your Commanding Officer, Christ Jesus the Lord. You'll be amazed at the increase in strength you've gained the next time you're squared off with the enemy.

Sixth, *give thanks*. God intends for you to rest in His unshakable, unchangeable provision. An excellent exercise to this end is His command that you "give thanks in all circumstances, for this is God's will for you in Christ Jesus" (1 Thess. 5:18) "All circumstances" includes being under spiritual attack. It doesn't have to make sense to you and, as stated before, it doesn't have to be what you're feeling. Just do it. "Thank you, my Father, that I am engaged in battle today." This is an affirmation to you and to your enemy that everything that touches you is with the knowledge and permission of your Heavenly Father and thus fits into His pattern of good for you. I can only imagine how this flings Satan and his emissaries headlong into anguished confusion. How much it pleases God is not left to our imagination. "Whoever hears my commands and obeys them, he is the one who loves me. He who loves me will be loved by my Father, and I, too, will love him and show myself to him" (John 14:21).

Seventh, *help someone else*. There is no more effective weapon against the doldrums than making a concentrated effort to lighten the load of someone else. You don't have to look very far to find someone who is in difficulty or distress whom you could encourage, comfort or help. "Carry each other's burdens, and in this way you will fulfill the law of Christ" (Gal. 6:2).

Take care not to use the opportunity of serving someone else as an open door to pour out your own woes. Carry that casserole to your sick neighbor with true concern for her and with cheerfulness in spite of your secret heartache. In this manner you fulfill the law of Christ and He will reward you with quietness, confidence and peace. "The fruit of righteousness will be peace; the effect of righteousness will be quietness and confidence forever" (Isa. 32:17). Try it, and watch the startled old serpent slither away.

You may have tactics of your own that can be added to this arsenal of suggestions, methods you have used with the help of God to procure control of troublesome thoughts. God works with each of us, like a loving Father, according to our bent or inclinations, yet always within the context of His written revelation to us. Let's return there for a final admonition that is not a suggestion but a command: "Finally, brothers, whatever is true, whatever is noble, whatever is right, whatever is pure, whatever is lovely, whatever is admirable—if anything is excellent or praiseworthy—think about such things" (Phil. 4:8).

Letting Go

We hear a lot these days about gaining "closure" of a hurtful past, and in the sense of bringing it to some sort of conclusion, I suppose the idea is valid. Closure may not be entirely profitable, though, depending on what it is you are closing out and what you are closing in.

My husband spent an entire summer doing work on the roof and soffits of our large front porch. (The roof was put on shoddily just before we purchased the house, and after six years we had numerous leaks and wood in various stages of rot.) Because our house is Victorian, there were gingerbread trim, moldings and other furbelows with which to contend in getting the job done, not to mention working high off the ground on extension ladders. Being the trooper he is, David singlehandedly completed the work, replacing not only part of the roof, but all of the soffit and fascia boards and crown molding. It was a huge undertaking, especially for someone who isn't a carpenter, and we all rejoiced when David nailed the last board in place, bringing closure to the space over the porch ceiling and also to that phase of the job.

That same night he applied the first coat of paint to the new wood, and then we all stood out in the street and admired his beautiful workmanship. Our "oohs" and "ahhs" were his reward for a job well done.

I wish that were the end of the story, but I'm afraid if we look ahead to the next evening the plot takes a most unexpected turn. There is David, back up the ladder, drilling, sawing and tearing at one of his securely nailed soffit boards. He has an audience of our entire family and a portion of the neighborhood.

Finally, he removes a large piece of the board and tosses it to the ground. The soffit is open again, his finished work undone. Why? Because, unknown to David, our family cat, Squeak, had climbed the ladder the day before, found an enticing hideaway between the porch ceiling and the roof and was accidentally sealed in. We couldn't find her all the next day and were finally alerted to her whereabouts late that afternoon by the frantic and mysterious meowing we heard. So much for closure.

Our pasts are a lot like that soffit. Even if we manage some sort of closure, it won't be permanent. We are composites of many factors, our pasts being one of those. How do we close the door on part of who we are? Why would we want to? We may discover later on that the closure we achieved closed in some hurtful emotion we didn't know was there, or closed out some person whose life could have been changed for good forever by our continued involvement in it. What can we do, then, to rid ourselves of the pain and dysfunction that weighs us down and causes us to stumble?

God wants us to release it, make an offering out of it, let it go. Sounds simple enough, doesn't it? You already know what I'm going to say, don't you? It is simple, but not easy. We have to really want to let go of it—that's the catch. So, who wouldn't want to release something as painful as our pasts? There are reasons why you may not. Let me explain.

My husband is a high-voltage electrician. He has both heard about and seen some horrendous accidents involving electricity, some caused by unsafe work habits of the victim, some caused by negligence of someone else, and a few caused by equipment malfunction. Whatever the cause, exposure of the human body to high-voltage current is sure to be damaging at the least and often is deadly. Sometimes a person's heart is thrown into fibrillation and he is badly burned and left unconscious. He still may survive, however, if many favorable conditions exist, including brevity of contact with the energized source. Another person exposed to the same voltage may be hopelessly doomed if one tragic, natural factor comes into play. Some call this "no-let-go arm paralysis." The person inadvertently touches the hot wire or equipment with his fingers or the palm of his hand and, instead of falling back and away from the source of shock, his muscles contract and he grasps it, unable to let go. His chances for survival are less than slim.

Some of us who have experienced severe emotional shock respond in much the same way. We're drawn into a "no-let-go" emotional paralysis that keeps us in contact with the source of our pain. This results in a wide range of emotional problems—from being disaffected and cantankerous to being debilitated by eating disorders, alcoholism, self-mutilation or depression. The body also suffers, not being created to withstand the long-term stress of unremitting rage. High blood pressure and an increased heart rate wear down our bodies and make us feel worn-out while it's happening. The effect on us spiritually is even more devastating, as our intense anger drives a wedge between us and the compassionate, loving God who alone can give us comfort and peace.

There is good news, though. For the Christian, the "no-let-go" syndrome is more *won't* than *can't*, for "I can do all things through Christ who strengthens me" (Phil. 4:13). It's just that letting go is so costly. God desires that I offer my suffering to Him as a unique sacrifice. In so doing, I will be privileged to give Him something no one else can give: my brokenness, my pain, my past. "The sacrifices of God are a broken spirit; a broken and contrite heart, O God, you will not despise" (Ps. 51:17). But I must also release the bitter-sweetness of being a victim. You know what I mean—that awful pleasure of being a person who must be delicately handled because "she has already been wounded, and we wouldn't want to do anything that would make it worse." No more expectations of special treatment. No more excuses for errant behavior. No more manipulation of people and circumstances because "she's had such a hard time of it, after all. Let's just let her have her way." No one leaves the altar of this sacrifice with those things in tow. They are all consumed by God's holy fire and all that is left are the ashes. "I will not . . . sacrifice a burnt offering that costs me nothing," King David said (1 Chron. 21:24). This offering will cost you everything.

Sound terrifying? If that were the end of it, it would be. But hear your Father's reassuring promise "to comfort all who mourn, . . . to bestow on them a crown of beauty instead of ashes, . . . and a garment of praise instead of a spirit of despair" (Isa. 61:2-3).

Why don't you make that appealing exchange with God right now? Ask Him to bind you to His holy altar and to extricate from your heart every tentacle and root of bitterness and self-pity. Yes, there may be some hurt involved with the process, but remember, He will not harm you; He plans to give you hope and a future. Now, visualize yourself kneeling with hands raised to heaven offering it all to Him, your suffering, your past and all the ugly roots of bitterness that He has so skillfully extracted. Imagine the purifying flame as it engulfs the offering, leaving your hands full of nothing but ashes. Then, in an act of total self-abandonment, offer Him even the ashes. And now, beloved Child of God, wait and see what wondrous delights He has in store for you.

Beauty for ashes! Who would have thought it possible?

Forgiveness

Dietrich Bonhoeffer was executed in 1945 for his outspoken defense of the Jews in Nazi Germany. Before his death, he wrote in a letter from prison to his fiancee, Maria: "Jesus Christ lived in the midst of His enemies. At the end all His disciples deserted Him. On the cross He was utterly alone, surrounded by evil-doers and mockers. For this cause He had come, to bring peace to the enemies of God. So the Christian, too, belongs not in the seclusion of a cloistered life but in the thick of foes."[4]

That is exactly where most of us are, at some time or other. Why? So that we might have the opportunity to imitate our Savior in forgiveness. In so doing, we are bringing peace to the enemies of God and to ourselves.

Many Christians seem to have misunderstood the true nature of forgiveness. The message we receive from the world is so contrary to God's picture of forgiveness in Christ that it is no wonder there is confusion even on the part of God's children, the forgiven ones. For example, an "expert" on the subject of child abuse was quoted in *Parade* magazine (August 28, 1993): "A particularly pernicious myth is that 'healing requires forgiveness' of the abuser. For the victim of emotional abuse, the most viable form of help is self-help—and a victim handicapped by the need to forgive is a handicapped helper indeed. . . . If you are a victim of emotional abuse, there can be no self-help until you learn to *self-reference*. That means developing your own standards, deciding for yourself what 'goodness' really is."

People actually pay money for such twaddle! Thank God that He has set the standard; He has demonstrated goodness and, consequently, we are not left to self-help devices. We can thank Him, too, that our Savior, who might have spurned us forever from His presence, carried in His pure heart a far different view of forgiveness. "Father, forgive them, for they do not know what they are doing," He breathed from the cross (Luke 23:34). It was Jesus, then, who not only spread the "pernicious myth" but gave birth to it. "Forgive us our debts, as we also have forgiven our debtors" was part of the prayer He modeled for us. Forgiveness wasn't just important to Jesus; it was the impetus of His life.

In the dozens of letters I have received from wounded, broken and often angry victims of "man's inhumanity to man," the writers' experience with forgiveness usually falls into one of three categories:

1. Those who have forgiven the perpetrators of their difficulty.
2. Those who question why they should.
3. Those who have tried to forgive and failed.

Let's take a quick look first at why we should forgive. God requires it. No ifs, ands or buts about it. "Bear with each other and forgive whatever grievances you may have against one another. Forgive as the Lord forgave you" (Col. 3:13). This command startled me as a young Christian. *How could God love me and yet require such a seeming impossibility from me?* I wondered. He knew the abuse I had endured at the hands of my mother and stepfather. They had never shown remorse or asked for forgiveness. Why, then, did I have to give it?

It wasn't long before I knew. "And when you stand praying, if you hold anything against anyone, forgive him, so that your Father in heaven may forgive you your sins" (Mark 11:25). "For if you forgive men when they sin against you, your heavenly Father will also forgive you. But if you do not forgive men their sins, your Father will not forgive your sins" (Matt. 6:14-15). It was necessary for me to forgive so that I could keep company with my Father. If I refused, my fellowship with Him would be broken, and so would my heart. Communion with Him meant more than anything to me. So I made up my mind that I would obey Him.

But I stumbled upon another problem, and that leads to the next question I want to address. "I tried to forgive but failed. Now what do I do?"

One explanation for a sense of failure is that the person who has made the choice to forgive is depending on feelings as a gauge of success. This was discussed in the section on "emotion vs. the will," so I won't wear you out with another long discourse here. Suffice it to say that forgiveness is not an emotion; it is a choice. You may, on some previous occasion, have experienced a sort of sentimental happiness when you chose to forgive someone of something, and so you came to confuse the feeling with the act. But the act of forgiveness exists perfectly well with no props of sentiment whatsoever. So you may be calling success failure without knowing it.

On the other hand, your difficulty with forgiveness might be, as was mine, because you have not yet recognized that, apart from the power of God, you can do nothing. I still remember gritting my teeth, clenching my fists and saying, "I'll forgive them if it kills me." Well, it didn't kill me, but I didn't forgive them either. I knew enough about God by that time that it was evident the problem was not with His edict but with my heart. In desperation I fell on my face before Him asking for His help. Then I saw the obvious. I am weak and in my flesh dwells no good thing. "My power is made perfect in weakness," God replied (2 Cor. 12:9). So I knew I had no strength of my own. "I can't do it myself, but I'm willing if You'll do it through me, my Lord."

He did do that work in me, and He'll do no less for you. Our fellowship is more than precious to Him. He has not designed any number of arbitrary rules in order to keep us miserable. He, the great Creator, knows exactly what is best for us emotionally, physically and spiritually. When He tells us to do something, it is not only for His good pleasure, but ultimately for ours as well.

Has someone gravely offended you? Have you, until now, refused to forgive either out of ignorance or because of rebellion in your heart? Where would you be today if the Savior had treated you thus?

"For I will forgive their wickedness and will remember their sins no more," declares the Lord (Heb. 8:12). "Arm yourselves also with the same attitude" (1 Pet. 4:1). You can't help it if someone, somehow, spoiled your past. But you can prevent an unforgiving spirit from destroying your future. It's your choice. I have every confidence you'll make the right one.

A Concluding Thought

Paul wrote to the believers at Colosse, "I want you to know how much I am struggling for you . . . and for all who have not met me personally. My purpose is that they may be encouraged in heart and united in love, so that they may have the full riches of complete understanding, in order that they may know the mystery of God, namely, Christ, in whom are hidden all the treasures of wisdom and knowledge" (Col. 2:1-3).

That is my heart and prayer for you, dear Child of God. May you find all the treasures of wisdom and knowledge hidden in Christ and apply them as you build and establish your home for the glory of God. For "by wisdom a house is built, and through understanding it is established; through knowledge its rooms are filled with rare and beautiful treasures" (Prov. 24:3-4).

Is that the kind of home for which you long? Then remember to trust in God's sovereignty, adopt an eternal perspective and heavenward focus, understand that your will is king and your emotions are servants, exercise control over your thought life, offer your suffering to God as a sacrifice, and allow Him to work forgiveness in your heart. Oh, and one more thing—don't ignore those little hills of white powder. Don't sweep them under the rug, either. Take them to the foot of the cross and leave them there.

et the past sleep, but let it sleep in the bosom of Christ, and go out into the irresistible future with Him.

—Oswald Chambers

4
Is There a Carpenter
In the House?

What a relief it was to be rid of those horrid little wood munchers! It took us a year to pay the exterminator's fee, during which time we gradually began again to beautify and restore our home. We had never had a large sum of money available for this purpose and now there was even less, but we carried on with slightly modified plans, determined to do what we could with what we had.

There remained one problem, though, and I would be remiss if I failed to tell you about it. You see, forcing the departure of these dastardly pests wasn't all we needed to do. They were gone and so were their little piles of sawdust, but they left behind damage and it was obvious something had to be done about it.

As far as the structural support of our house was concerned, the massive beams and joists remained virtually unscathed. Inside the house, however, was another story.

The floor of our entry hall is composed of random-width tongue-and-groove pine boards. This apparently is the preferred diet of powder post beetles. While much of the floor was untouched by the invaders, some of it was damaged, and a few of the boards were almost completely gutted. Those, which were located just inside the front door, were about as sound to walk on as an empty pastry shell. Without a doubt, they would have to be replaced.

As I've already told you, my husband is not a carpenter by trade. The poor man knows that whenever he embarks on a woodworking project it's going to be a slow, tedious job. The fact that he is facing difficult work never stops him, though. Tenacity is his middle name.

I must confess I am a bit more fainthearted than he. The thought of having to endure one more unexpected undertaking of this magnitude discouraged me. *Couldn't we just cover this mess with a lovely carpet and hope for the best?* I wondered.

I admit it was not a brilliant idea, but a body does get tired. Anyway, I never would have voiced it to my husband, the perfectionist. So the messy, inconvenient work was begun. I won't bore you with the details. You only need to know that the damaged wood was finally removed and the new wood installed, with excellent results. Now, we not only have a more beautiful floor, but our guests and loved ones are no longer in danger of falling through when they visit. It was well-spent effort, I must concede.

As I examined a piece of the wood David extracted from the floor, I was astonished to discover how severely damaged it actually was. Those insects had tunneled back and forth through the entire board, leaving only wafer-thin layers in between. I could poke my finger all the way through in spots. Imagine how dangerous that was underfoot!

It caused me to reflect on the plight of some of God's wounded, impaired children. Oh, they've been accepted in the Beloved. They've done battle with the enemy too. They overcame, against all odds, all manner of onslaught, abuse or neglect only to discover that, for all the effort and personal expense, they've been left with a significant amount of damage that is as varied as we individuals vary. It may show up as an eating disorder, or as an alcohol-, drug- or other addiction-related problem. In some it may exhibit itself in bizarre spending habits, self-mutilation, promiscuity or any of a myriad of methods of self-destruction. Every year, it seems, we learn of some "new" or heretofore unknown behavior disorder, and God's children are not immune.

Are you one of those scarred and weakened dear ones for whom Christ died? Are you asking the questions that have so often been asked of me: "What is wrong with me that I have been left with these problems? Why hasn't God healed me?"

My heart spills over with sympathy for you as did the heart of the prophet Jeremiah for his people: "My sorrow is beyond healing, my heart is faint within me. . . . For the brokenness of the daughter of my people I am broken; I mourn, dismay has taken hold of me. Is there no balm in Gilead? Is there no physician there? Why then has not the health of the daughter of my people been restored?" (Jer. 8:18, 21-22, NAS).

Was Jeremiah lamenting because there *was* no balm, no physician, no restoration? No. He wept over a far more appalling set of circumstances. There was indeed a healing balm readily available for the restoration of God's people. They simply had refused to appropriate it. Why? You won't like this answer. I don't care much for it myself, but it's the truth. Their own sin kept them from the services of the Great Physician.

Now let me clarify something before we continue. If at some point in your past you have been violated, abused, reviled and maligned, you are not in the least responsible for that. You are not dirtied, demeaned or devalued, in spite of the way you were left feeling. There is absolutely no guilt in you as a result of being a victim. The one who victimized you sinned against you and against God. It was his sin-nature at work that violated you, and he will answer to God for it.

Having clarified that, we must understand something else: even the sweetest, most pitiful victim on the face of the earth also possesses a sin-nature. And while this had nothing to do with the terrible abuse perpetrated on her, it often has everything to do with her response to it. This sinful response syndrome was discussed extensively in chapter 3, but I'm suggesting to you now that its results can be so far-reaching as to cause an unconscious unwillingness to be healed. When this occurs, the victim's *own sin* is contributing to the perpetuation of her damage. She has bound the loving, healing hand of God and is therefore without remedy.

Listen to God's response to Jeremiah's heart-rending questioning: "For thus says the Lord, 'Your wound is incurable, and your injury is serious. There is no one to plead your cause; no healing for your sore, no recovery for you. . . . Why do you cry out over your injury? Your pain is incurable. *Because your iniquity is great and your sins are numerous*, I have done these things to you" (Jer. 30:12-13, 15, NAS, emphasis mine).

God never minces words, does He? That is because His love for us is so deep, so pure, that He wants nothing but the best for us. He desires to set us free, and that can be accomplished only by our knowing the truth, including the truth about ourselves. We victims are sinners, too, and it is our own sinfulness that hinders our recovery.

I am neither a psychologist nor a theologian, but I have observed at least four common threads that run through the destructive behavior patterns of those who have sustained damage. I think you will agree that they each contain an element of sin or rebellion against God.

1. *A refusal to recognize or accept authority.* Often, the individual was violated by a person who had authority over her. This made her more vulnerable to the abuse than she otherwise would have been. A little girl is under the authority of her father. She also depends on him for protection, provision and love. If he is abusive to her, she is more confused and hurt than if a perfect stranger had abused her. The natural response of that little girl, then, would be to reject all authority in her life, thereby hoping to prevent any more such grievous injury. Notice I said *natural response*. The Scriptures refer to our sin nature as the "natural man" (1 Cor. 2:14, KJV). Our natural inclinations are always away from God and His will for us. Rejection of authority is rejection of God, and it is sin no matter how "understandable" that response may be.

2. *The compelling desire to be in complete control of both circumstances and people.* It doesn't take a behavioral scientist to understand why a victim of abuse would respond with this compulsion. She may have endured horrifying circumstances over

which she had no control. Consequently, she is terrified of ever losing control again. Ironically, the desire for control often sets itself up as despot and the victim becomes the out-of-control slave, all the while believing the delusion that she is finally in control after all. What a tragedy.

Look at the case of the anorexic teenager, for example. At an age when body image is everything, she perceives that hers would be improved by the loss of a few pounds. She may or may not be overweight. Perception, not reality, is the force that rules.

She decides to "take control" of the situation. In a few weeks she has successfully taken off some weight. Her friends notice. She's encouraged by their comments. Something clicks in her head as she realizes that she actually made something happen. She is in control of her weight. Furthermore, no one can take that control from her. And if she could lose a few pounds with so little effort, she can probably lose a few more.

She can, of course, and she does. Before she knows it, the obsession with her weight is in charge and she no longer is making or is able to make conscious choices. She's heading straight into a death trap while on cruise control. She can't stop herself, doesn't *want* to stop herself and has no idea, for the longest time, of the kind of trouble she's in. Often, by the time she does know, it's too late.

3. *The use of secrecy and deception to cover up erratic behavior.* This is similar to my wish to "just cover this mess with a lovely carpet and forget about it." The person is confused, frightened and ashamed. She believes she can stop her peculiar behavior anytime she decides to do so, but until then she will concoct one elaborate scheme after another to keep anyone from finding out about it. The anorexic secretly disposes of food she has pretended to eat. The compulsive overeater hides food and eats in secret. The alcoholic mother begins drinking as soon as her children leave for school, then attempts to cover the smell of booze with perfume before her husband returns home from work. The prescription drug addict comes up with one new

complaint of pain after another until her physician grows suspicious. Then she switches doctors and starts all over again. There is never any peace in these deception-driven lives.

Inevitably, whether the person is a master deceiver or a novice, the truth eventually closes in and, when confronted, she has only one thing left to do—she must find an explanation for her behavior. This leads to observation number four.

4. *Placing blame on the one(s) who caused the damage in the first place.* "I can't help it. You know what (name of violator here) did to me. It still affects me. I'll never get over it. It's so unfair!"

Now please don't be offended and turn away. I know this hurts. I've been there. But I care for you far too much to not tell you the truth. Your future and the future of your loved ones depend on it. It is Christ who compels me. Will you not listen to Him?

Blaming others usually also involves surrounding oneself with as many sympathizers as possible. These people are selected carefully for their availability, their attentiveness and their seemingly unending willingness to commiserate. If one of these "confidants" begins to show signs of weariness or of wanting the victim to take responsibility for her own behavior, she may be quickly replaced with a fresh face of consolation.

It is of utmost importance to understand that I am not implying that this person is not really suffering, or has not endured tremendous abuse, or is not presently severely incapacitated as a result of someone else's despicable behavior. Nor am I suggesting the need for comfort and compassion is not a legitimate human need.

What you must see, though, is the futility of wasting all that time and energy on blame and self-absorption instead of pressing on with the restoration work. You can blame your parents, your grandparents, that neighbor or teacher or anyone else who harmed you, but in the end where will you be? At the same place with the same damage.

Suppose my husband, upon discovering that our floor had been turned into something akin to papier-mache, had responded, "Just look at this mess! It isn't our fault that this happened. We were completely innocent. We never consented to letting those pests into our house. Why should we have to do all this work? It's an outrage! I won't do it. It isn't my responsibility."

He could have chosen to rant and rave all day long, or for a lifetime for that matter. And we can do the same thing about our damaged lives. We can struggle, cry and fight. When nothing seems to work we can spend the rest of our lives pointing at the damage and wailing, "It isn't fair. It's not my fault." Meanwhile, nothing is being done about the actual damage. We have established a fact but we haven't effected a solution.

The biggest tragedy of all is that the next generation—our beloved offspring—will end up pointing at their own damage and singing the same dirge.

And on it goes. "You . . . bring the punishment for the fathers' sins into the laps of their children after them" (Jer. 32:18). But it doesn't have to be that way. There is One, a carpenter by trade (Mark 6:1-3), who came not only to redeem you but to restore you as well.

You see, every soul comes to God damaged. Damage results from sin—our own sin and the sin of others. This results in inestimable sorrow and grief.

But *all* of that sin and sorrow, regardless of its source, was dealt with at Calvary. Listen to the Scriptures describe what our Messiah, the miracle-working carpenter, has done: "Surely our griefs He Himself bore, and our sorrows He carried; yet we ourselves esteemed Him smitten of God, and afflicted. But He was pierced through for our transgressions, He was crushed for our iniquities; the chastening for our peace fell upon Him, and by His scourging we are healed" (Isa. 53:4-5, NAS).

Look at those verses carefully. For our peace and for the healing of our sin-sick souls, the Son of God was smitten, afflicted, pierced, crushed and scourged. If that wasn't enough, in order to eradicate the effects of *other's* sins on our lives, He bore our griefs and carried our sorrows! He did it all. Redemption *and* restoration were the finished work of our Lord Jesus.

So what is left for you to do? Read the instructions God gave to Moses for the Israelites as they were being hotly pursued by Pharaoh's army: "Do not be afraid. Stand firm and you will see the deliverance the LORD will bring you today. . . . The LORD will fight for you; you need only to be still" (Ex. 14:13-14). Where is the struggle in that? Whose energy is being spent? What is the promised result?

Have you been thinking all along that you must somehow repair your damage? Why, you could no more do that than our foyer floor could have restored itself! God must do the restoring. What you must do, Daughter, is yield. I'm not pretending that yielding is easy. It is the hardest thing in the world. Considering our natures, it is *impossible*, "but with God all things are possible" (Matt. 19:26).

Yielding means absolute relinquishment of everything: every known sin, every perceived "right," every desire for restitution, every notion that you can do it yourself. It means being still. It means not being in control anymore. It means not covering up anymore. And it means giving up the blaming and becoming accountable for your own behavior.

The Master Carpenter is at work in you. Will you lie passive and still in His capable, loving arms, availing yourself of His great skill and power? He never takes a wrong measurement, makes an inaccurate cut, bends a nail or leaves rough edges. He isn't too busy for the small jobs, and He's never overwhelmed by even the most serious damage. "I am the LORD, the God of all mankind. Is anything too hard for me?" (Jer. 32:27). It makes no difference how weakened you are, for He has said, "My power is made perfect in weakness" (2 Cor. 12:9). He knows exactly what and where your weaknesses are and He still wants you. His love for you remains unaffected. "I have chosen you and have not rejected you. So do not fear, for I am with you; do not be dismayed, for I am your God. I will strengthen you and help you; I will uphold you with my righteous right hand" (Isa. 41:9-10).

You may wonder, "But won't it be painful to submit myself to this restorative work?" Remember, the actual work was completed 2,000 years ago and, yes, it was immeasurably, indescribably painful for the One who submitted to it. He never opened His mouth, though, because it was to accomplish that work on your behalf that He came.

The appropriation of that restoration to our lives is also a painful process because it hurts our selfish natures to yield. It also hurts to be told the truth about ourselves: "Because your iniquity is great and your sins are numerous, I have done these things to you." All the rebellion, control, deception and blaming must be stripped off like old layers of varnish. And it is intensely painful.

Oh, but our wise Father, who in helping us must sometimes hurt us, will never harm us. "A bruised reed he will not break, and a smoldering wick he will not snuff out, till he leads justice to victory" (Matt. 12:20). Remember those plans He has "to prosper you and not to harm you" (Jer. 29:11).

Jesus was sent to be close to the brokenhearted (Ps. 34:18), to bind up their wounds (Isa. 61:1) and to heal them (Ps. 147:3). As an example to us He came in perfect submission to the will of His Father. He did not hold back anything but offered Himself up for us all. In urging us to do likewise, He comforts us again and again with these words: "Do not be afraid." "Do not fear." "Fear not."

Let go of your anxiety and resistance. You have God's unshakable word that He will not harm you. You're His beloved child. He delights in you. Do you imagine He has told you a lie?

I am frequently asked, "How long does healing take? Does it happen all at once, or is it a process?"

The answer lies in another question: "How long will it take you to yield?" It may take only two hours for a surgeon to remove a tumor from your body, but if it took you a year to decide to have the surgery, then the process was a year and two hours long. Could you then complain that the surgeon was slow? Of course not. He worked wonders for you once you yielded yourself to him. The process was in your overcoming your fear of surgery, or your lack of trust in the surgeon.

Some of us yield quickly in some areas, more slowly in others. That is why it is confusing and foolish to compare ourselves to any other of God's children (2 Cor. 10:12). Our focus is to be on the LORD, who "is not slow in keeping his promise" (2 Pet. 3:9). He is always ready to work His good and perfect will in our lives, and He is not a respecter of persons. Each child of God is equally loved and shares equally in His power.

Oswald Chambers wrote, "Never sympathize with a soul who finds it difficult to get to God. God is not to blame. . . . If we make our inability a barrier to obedience, it means we are telling God there is something He has not taken into account. Complete weakness and dependence will always be the occasion for the Spirit of God to manifest his power."[1]

So what's the holdup? We deceive ourselves into believing that we're yielded completely to God when in reality we are holding something back. We may not even realize it, but we are.

This is where counseling can be effective. God has many gifted, well-trained men and women who can be of invaluable service in helping you peel off layer after layer of self-deception, exposing the unyielded areas of your life. Armed with the wisdom of God's Word, prayer and your willingness to know the truth about yourself, a godly counselor can make a real difference in the progress of your restoration. The counselor's gift of comfort and compassion also can be beneficial as you seek God's face in the matter.

But do not forget that for every counselor who will guide you in truth, there are probably five who will "take you captive through hollow and deceptive philosophy" (Col. 2:8) and who have, after all, a vested interest in keeping you right where you are. The longer they have you digging around your graveyard of memories, pulling up the skeletal remains of every painful incident in your past, the more you'll need counseling and, to be sure, they'll be there for you. Oh, do be careful. There is danger in that psycho-babble claptrap.

Also, be aware that your desire for constant comfort and sympathy can become an insatiable appetite. We each like to think of ourselves as a special case. "The first lesson of life is to burn our own smoke; that is, not to inflict on outsiders our personal sorrows and petty morbidness; not to keep thinking of ourselves as exceptional cases" (James Russell Lowell).[2] We enjoy our misery. God is not in that. He lifts us up and out of ourselves. As George MacDonald put it, "All the doors that lead inward to the secret place of the Most High are doors outward—out of self—out of smallness—out of wrong."[3]

Before seeking counsel anywhere else, why don't you get on your knees before the Wonderful Counselor? Tell Him you want to be restored. Ask Him to show you the truth about yourself so that you might become fully yielded to His control. Wait patiently before Him. Trust Him. Abandon yourself to Him. Relax your tightly clenched fists and relinquish all to Him. There is no one on earth who knows you as He knows you. Nothing is hidden from His eyes.

Do you need compassion? "Return to the LORD your God, for he is gracious and compassionate, slow to anger, and abounding in love" (Joel 2:13). "'With everlasting kindness I will have compassion on you,' says the LORD your Redeemer" (Isa. 54:8).

Are you longing to be comforted? "For this is what the LORD says: . . . 'As a mother comforts her child, so will I comfort you'" (Isa. 66:12-13). "Praise be to the God and Father of our LORD Jesus Christ, the Father of compassion and the God of all comfort, who comforts us in all our troubles, so that we can comfort those in any trouble with the comfort we ourselves received from God" (2 Cor. 1:3-4).

Do you fear the future? Are you running from your past? Why, dear Child, when the Creator of the universe protects you from behind and before? "For the LORD will go before you, the God of Israel will be your rear guard" (Isa. 52:12).

Are you willing to put your damage behind you and to be restored? He is more than willing to do it for you, though He knows all about you. "I have seen his ways, but I will heal him; I will guide him and restore comfort to him" (Isa. 57:18).

Be still. Permit the Savior to make evident in your life the healing that was purchased long ago with His own blood. "For I am confident of this very thing, that He who began a good work in you will perfect it until the day of Christ Jesus" (Phil. 1:6, NAS).

> Come ye disconsolate, where'er ye languish;
> Come to the mercy-seat, fervently kneel
> Here bring your wounded hearts, here tell your anguish;
> Earth has no sorrow that Heaven cannot heal.
> Joy of the desolate, light of the straying,
> Hope, when all others die, fadeless and pure!
> Here speaks the Comforter, tenderly saying,
> Earth has no sorrow that Heaven cannot cure.
>
> — Thomas Moore

*T*herefore, if you are offering your gift at the altar and there remember that your brother has something against you, leave your gift there in front of the altar. First go and be reconciled to your brother; then come and offer your gift.

—*Matthew 5:23*

5
Help! Someone's Been Hurt!

"The pests are gone and the damage has been repaired. Now will you please help me redecorate my living room?" That's what you're thinking, isn't it?

I understand. There is nothing I would like better, but first things must come first. We'll be dealing with those fun, easy projects later. For now we are compelled to continue the serious work of self-examination and relinquishment. Why? Because the most beautiful ornamentation our homes will ever know is the mind of Jesus revealed in us. All the gorgeous embellishments money can buy will not make up for its lack. Nothing else will give your family the joyous advantage you so desperately want it to have. If hearth and home are somehow snatched away, your dear ones can still have the shelter of your pure, unassailable spirit. Isn't that what you really want? Then roll up your sleeves and prepare your heart. Some hard truths lie before us.

I've already told you more than you ever wanted to know about the extermination of powder post beetles from our house and the subsequent restoration of the pulverized floor. As difficult and drawn out as the process was, we realized how fortunate we were to have caught the problem when we did. Had it gone on much longer, we're sure to have sustained substantial structural damage and, worse, someone might have been injured by stepping right through the dilapidated boards.

The parallel story of my life isn't quite as simple. Almost as soon as I entered a relationship with God through Jesus Christ, I became aware of the presence within me of the ensnaring pests we discussed previously. Bitterness, resentment, hatred, anger and self-pity were eating away at me, preventing spiritual growth and thereby causing inestimable damage to my soul. My spirit, too, had been brutalized by the various sins of others. I was damaged goods, all right. But God began His transforming work in my heart and, as quickly as I would yield each area to Him, restored my wounded soul and spirit. It was nothing less than a miracle. He, not I, performed the entire work. My part was only in saying (and meaning), "Thy will be done."

So, there was glorious victory and we all lived happily ever after, right? Well, yes and no. Every victory we experience as Christians is significant to God. Victory is always His desire for us. He gave His only Son that we might obtain it. He's on our side.

It is for that very reason that God is never satisfied with our past victories, however great they may have been. He is constantly urging us, escorting us on to the next. And so, when He knew I was ready, God brought me face-to-face with a horrifying truth: before I had completely yielded to His meticulous restoration of my life, someone went crashing through my weakness and was injured.

Early one morning as I listened to His voice, God showed me. Thinking He surely couldn't mean what I thought I had heard, I turned my ear to Him again. "Therefore, if you are offering your gift at the altar and there remember that your brother has something against you, leave your gift there in front of the altar. First go and be reconciled to your brother; then come and offer your gift" (Matt. 5:23-24).

The Holy Spirit immediately put His convicting finger on my heart and I knew someone had something against me. I didn't want to believe it, but I had no choice. It was true, and the truth sickened me.

Ever since coming to Christ I had witnessed to my mother of Him. At first it was not out of sincere concern for her soul, but because I had learned witnessing was expected of me by other Christians. As God began transforming me, however, and especially after He worked out the forgiveness of her in my heart, I truly desired to see her rescued from sin by my lovely Savior. She wouldn't listen, though. She wanted no part of me or my God.

This baffled me until that momentous morning when I read Matthew 5:23-24. Then God revealed to me the ugly reality: my pride had kept me from loving my mother as a daughter should. Even after my conversion I had continued treating her with a lack of respect. My tone of voice, even my body language, had told her exactly how I felt about her, in spite of what I said. I had been an offense to her, a stumbling block in the path that led to Christ. I was devastated. And I knew that God would not reveal another thing to me until I had obeyed this Word. It seemed to me He was asking too much this time. Why should I care if my mother sustained injury? Hadn't she inflicted most of my damage, after all? Who could blame me for refusing this one instruction?

Who, indeed?

The One who forgives all my sins and heals all my diseases, who redeems my life from the pit and crowns me with love and compassion, who satisfies my desires with good things (Ps. 103:3-5)—*He* could blame me. To Him I am responsible. Never will I be held accountable for the injustices committed by my mother. I am accountable, though, for my response to them.

God revealed it to me with loving-kindness and merciful tenderness. He knows my frame, that I am dust, but that didn't change the requirement. I could do as He said or I could disobey. Which would it be?

Before I tell you the rest of the story, let's stop for a moment and think about you. You knew I'd come around to that eventually, didn't you?

Jesus' words in Matthew 5:23-24 weren't recorded just for me. They are there for every child of God. He doesn't want us bringing our sacrificial offerings to His altar while blocking the way of someone else. However damaged we are, we are without excuse. It is the sin of pride (which is at the heart of our sin nature) that causes us to balk at this requirement: "First go and be reconciled to your brother; then come and offer your gift." Notice how the Father is urging you to do two right things: 1) be reconciled and 2) come and offer your gift. He isn't rejecting you or your gift. Never did He say, "Get away from my holy altar, you filthy sinner! I don't want your tainted offering." He could have said that and been justified. But He *wants* your offering. Oh, how He wants it! So He tells you what to do that He might be able to receive it. And then—this is terribly important—He again does the work in you to make your obedience not just possible, but certain! "For we are God's workmanship, created in Christ Jesus to do good works, which God *prepared in advance for us to do*" (Eph. 2:10, emphasis mine). He planned in advance, ages ago, before He spoke the worlds into existence, how He would enable you to do all that He requires.

O obedience, where is thy sting? The sting is in the response of our stubborn wills. The balm is in complete abandonment of our wills to God.

Oswald Chambers explained it this way: "The battle is lost or won in the secret places of the will before God. . . . Every now and again, not often, but sometimes, God brings us to a point of climax. That is the Great Divide in the Life; from that point we either go towards a more and more dilatory and useless type of Christian life, or we become more and more ablaze for the glory of God—My Utmost for *His* Highest."[1]

Which will it be for you? Will you abandon your own will, embrace the will of God and obey His decree?

Before continuing I must clarify something. You may not presently sense God speaking to you in Matthew 5:23-24. This could be true for a number of reasons. If you have not yet entered God's family, He won't be dealing with you at all except in the critical area of salvation. Or, if you are His child, you may be one of those rare, sensitive spirits who responded so quickly to God's offer of restoration and healing that no one had a chance to "fall through" your damage.

It also could be that you are still in the "extermination" or "restoration" phases and are not yet ready to hear God on this. Your Heavenly Father is full of wisdom; He'll never bombard you with light for which you are not ready, and He knows perfectly when you are ready.

Therefore, if what I've been telling you makes no sense to you or brings confusion rather than conviction, don't fret over it. Simply allow God to continue His marvelous work in your life. Trust His leading and wait patiently before Him.

If, on the other hand, you sense the convicting power of the Holy Spirit, don't resist Him, however painful it may be. You are at the "Great Divide" and you must obey. Do not delay or harden your heart. Your future walk with God depends on it. Your effectiveness as a wife and mother depends on it. The receiving of your offering by God depends on it. Do you have an idea of all that hangs on the thread of your obedience?

Having said that with such emphasis, permit me to point out another item of great importance: you are not in the least responsible for the convicting work of God. Trust Him for that; He will do it. You needn't spend time and energy dredging up offended persons from your past. If you are sincerely willing to obey your Father in this matter, the person(s) will be brought to mind with no effort whatsoever on your part. It will happen as naturally as oil rising to the surface of water. In fact, you won't be able to prevent it from happening.

Listen to the wise and powerful words of Oswald Chambers on the subject:

> "If when you come to the altar, there you remember that your brother has anything against you," not—if you rake up something by a morbid sensitiveness, but—"If thou rememberest," that is, if it is brought to your conscious mind by the Spirit of God: "first be reconciled to thy brother and then come and offer thy gift." Never object to the intense

sensitiveness of the Spirit of God in you when He is edu-
cating you down to the scruple.

"First be reconciled to thy brother . . ." Our Lord's direction
is simple, "first be reconciled." Go back the way you came,
go the way indicated to you by the conviction given at the
altar; have an attitude of mind and a temper of soul to the
one who has something against you that makes reconcilia-
tion as natural as breathing. Jesus does not mention the
other person, He says—*you* go. There is no question of
your rights. The stamp of the saint is that he can waive his
own rights and obey the Lord Jesus.

"And then come and offer thy gift!" The process is clearly
marked. First, the heroic spirit of self-sacrifice, then the
sudden checking by the sensitiveness of the Holy Spirit,
and the stoppage at the point of conviction, then the way
of obedience to the word of God, constructing an unblam-
able attitude of mind and temper to the one with whom
you have been in the wrong; then the glad, simple, unhin-
dered offering of your gift to God.[2]

So your spirit, being sensitive to God's Spirit, is convicted
concerning an offended brother. This person could be a parent,
a child, a sibling, a spouse, a friend, a neighbor. It could even
be, as it was in my case, the person who either through carelessness or an act of the will wounded you! But it matters not,
for God has spoken. So what is your next step?

Pray for courage and wisdom. Tell God what He already
knows but wants to hear from you—that you can't do it. He is
more than willing to do it through you. "Because the Sovereign
Lord helps me, I will not be disgraced. Therefore have I set my
face like a flint, and I know I will not be put to shame"
(Isa. 50:7).

Next, if possible, set up a time when you can meet with the
person face-to-face. To look that person in the eye while confessing your sin and asking forgiveness requires valiance and
humility and speaks volumes concerning your sincerity. If the
person lives thousands of miles away and reunion is impossible,

a telephone call is acceptable. It might be much less effective than an in-person conversation, but God does not ask the impossible of us, so trust Him to make it work.

Whatever you do, don't allow distance to prevent your obedience. As you let time go by, you will minimize your offenses in your own mind and harden your heart to God's Spirit. Your delay will become disobedience and you will be robbed of joy and rest. "Today, if you hear his voice, do not harden your hearts . . . . That is why I was angry with that generation, and I said, 'Their hearts are always going astray, and they have not known my ways.' So I declared an oath in my anger, 'They shall never enter my rest'" (Heb. 3:7-8, 10-11). God requires this of you because His purpose for you is that you might prosper, and He desires to give you rest. Don't allow pride and temporary ease to rob you of these everlasting blessings.

The least-effective method of asking forgiveness would be to write a letter. Without the aid of your facial expressions, gestures or tone of voice, a different meaning can unwittingly be assigned to your words. The recipient may read between the lines a message far different from what you intended. Furthermore, a letter documents your offenses and could be used against you. Also, a written confession does not require a response. You may never receive the forgiveness you are seeking. Before writing a letter, ask God to give you the opportunity to call or meet with the person you have wronged.

When the time does arrive, honestly state your offense and make your request for forgiveness clear. Don't talk too much. The more you talk, the more you'll attempt to make excuses for your offensive behavior. You may even try to spread some of the blame on others. Don't do it. Only *you* are responsible for your behavior.

Remember, the purpose of the meeting is not to smooth things over but to confess and request forgiveness. Leave the results to God, realizing that you may not receive forgiveness in spite of going in a spirit of genuine humility and repentance (though this is rare). In such a case, pray for the offended person and continue to live in such a manner that he will believe your sincerity. God's Spirit will do a convicting work in his heart. You have done what God required of you.[3]

When I realized that my wrong attitudes had been an offense to my mother, I did everything possible to persuade myself that it wasn't so. But it *was* so. God loved me too much to let me get away from it.

Finally, I agreed with Him about it, but I still wasn't feeling sorry for it. Of course, he never asked me to "feel" anything, but there is a place for godly sorrow, as described in 2 Corinthians 7:10: "Godly sorrow brings repentance . . . . See what this godly sorrow has produced in you: what earnestness, what eagerness to clear yourselves, what indignation, what alarm, what longing, what concern, what readiness to see justice done." When I understood that I could go to my mother as a genuine repentant only if I were truly sorry, I asked God to help me. He did.

I began to see my mother through God's eyes, realizing to my horror that my ill treatment of her was my very treatment of Jesus Christ. Reviewing in my mind my sharp words, my pious attitude, my insensitivity to her needs—in short, my many sins against her and against God—left me broken and terribly, fervently sorry.

So with God's help I called her on the phone and asked if I might come by for a visit. "What for?" she asked in her customarily angry voice. "I'd like to talk to you about something," I replied. "How about tomorrow afternoon?" I held my breath in suspense. My heart pounded out the seconds as I awaited her response. "I guess that'll be all right," she muttered.

So the next day I went. The only way I know to describe my mother is in degrees of hardness. "Flint" comes to mind. That is probably as close as you can get to a word picture of her. Imagine my fear and trembling! But when I looked into her cold, sin-hardened face that day I began to experience, for the first time, a deep awareness of her suffering combined with the desire to relieve it. In other words, God poured His compassion through my heart. So I began to state my cause. "Mother, you know I am a Christian now. I've spoken to you many times about my Savior," I began.

She refused me eye contact but I could tell she was listening.

"I understand now why you never wanted to hear what I had to say. You see, God has convicted me that I have sinned against Him and against you because I haven't shown you the respect due you as my mother. I've displayed a rebellious attitude in my manner of speaking to you and in my lack of a loving spirit toward you. I'm here today to ask you, will you forgive me?" She glanced up at me with a fleeting look of shock, then averted her eyes again.

After a heart-arresting silence she replied gruffly, "I don't have anything to forgive you for." My heart sank. I took a deep breath and repeated, nearly word for word, my original confession and request for forgiveness.

This time some of the hardness melted from her face. Her lighted cigarette sat neglected in the ashtray, becoming a tenuous gray cylinder. I waited and waited and waited. She looked at me once again, looked away, took a long puff on what was left of her cigarette and then snuffed out the nub. She exhaled the smoke in a long, drawn-out sigh.

I was silently praying. The smoke was burning my eyes and nostrils and I began to question why I had ever come. My hope was vanishing more quickly than was the smoke from that stuffy little room. Then my mother spoke.

"Of course I'll forgive you," she said. That was all. No trumpet fanfares, no choir of angels, no fireworks. But something happened that day, something mysterious and miraculous and monumental. If you listened very intently you might have been able to hear it: the sound of a wall crashing down. Not, as I had very much hoped, the wall between my mother and me. For whatever reason, God didn't permit that. My mother had never been able to love me, and in the few short months she had left, never would.

But the wall came down between my mother and the Lord Jesus Christ. Just weeks after that afternoon of confession and forgiveness, my mother knelt down with my pastor in that same little room where I had been molested all of my growing up years, and she received salvation through the blood of Christ. Then the angels were singing! Praise God for the infinite grace that reaches into even the vilest, most detestable stations on earth and transforms their inhabitants into children of the King of Kings!

That year I experienced the only Christmas I would ever have with a sober mother. And while her attitude toward me did not noticeably change, I was permitted to see her finally lose her addiction to alcohol, which helped confirm for me the sincerity of her faith in Christ. Less than a year later, five days before my fourth child was born, God took her home.

How thankful I was, then, that He had chastened me so severely because of my injurious offenses! How glad I was that His Word is sharper than any two-edged sword! How delighted I was that He had led me in paths of righteousness for His name's sake!

God does lead us in paths of righteousness that we might glorify and avoid bringing reproach to His Name. We must seek to own no ulterior motives. It is only human to want to be loved and have relationships restored. I admit that I went to my mother's house that day not only to do the will of God but because I cherished the hope that I could somehow make her love me. God showed me that my expectations were not the important thing; my obedience was. That is what is meant by complete self-abandonment. And isn't that a blessed relief? When we leave the outcome totally to Him (and we have to do that anyway), the results are always far more glorious than we could have imagined—far different, too.

For whatever reason, God did not ordain a conciliation between my mother and me. We must always keep in mind that there are far greater issues at stake in God's economy than those we see, feel and pray about. He sees and knows *everything* about them and has promised that "to those who love God, who are called according to His plan, everything that happens fits into a pattern for good" (Rom. 8:28, Phillips). Consequently, we walk by faith, not by sight, no matter how hopeless our circumstances appear.

Everything certainly appeared hopeless to me when my mother died. I was brokenhearted, knowing that the possibility for a loving earthly relationship between us was forever over. It grieved me. The loss I felt was unspeakable.

It wasn't long, though, before God showed me how childish I was to imagine I could dictate to Him how He should respond to my obedience. Smitten, I brought to the holy altar all my desires for a mother and offered them up to Him, to do with as He chose. (Remember, according to Matthew 5:23-24, I was free once again to bring my offerings before Him.)

In the Old Testament, whenever God received a sacrificial offering it was immediately consumed by fire, leaving nothing but ashes. Those remaining ashes, which certainly appeared ugly and useless, were evidence that the offering was acceptable to God. His seal of approval is seldom the pomp and glitter we seek. And it nearly always involves the thing we most dread: waiting. We never wait, however, without an infallible promise to bank on—His promise to "bestow on them a crown of beauty instead of ashes" (Isa. 61:3).

Three years after I offered my desire for a mother's love to God, He fulfilled that precious promise in my life. He gave to me the most unexpected, unimaginable gift of a lifetime—a spiritual mother. She has since taught and corrected and comforted and loved me as my birth mother never could have done. What joy comes by following the will of God and leaving the results to Him!

So, how about you? Has some soul for whom Christ died suffered harm or injury because of you? Have you stood in the way of someone's coming to Christ? Did your weakened spirit splinter under the load before the healing work of your Great Physician was completed? Are you remembering that someone has something against you? Then go, Child. Go now and do God's bidding.

Don't be concerned about what people think about *you*. Think only of their impression of the Savior. Submit your will to the will of God; go in the power of His Spirit and with the attitude of His Son, who made Himself *nothing* for our sakes. Go wherever He asks.

Then rejoice, for you will have given to God the offering He most desires: the pouring out of yourself. Make your way to the altar and make that costly sacrifice. What do you think will spring forth from those ashes after you've been spent and poured out? "Eye hath not seen, nor ear heard, neither have entered into the heart of man, the things which God hath prepared for them that love Him" (1 Cor. 2:9, KJV).

Just you wait and see.

> We praise and bless Thee, gracious Lord,
> Our Savior kind and true,
> For all the old things passed away,
> For all Thou hast made new.
>
> But yet how much must be destroyed
> How much renewed must be,
> Ere we can fully stand complete
> In likeness, Lord, to Thee!
>
> Thou only Thou, must carry on
> The work Thou hast begun;
> Of Thine own strength Thou must impart
> In Thine own ways to run.
>
> So shall we faultless stand at last
> Before Thy Father's throne;
> The blessednesss forever ours,
> The glory all Thine own!
> — Charles John Spitta

If anyone loves me, he will obey my teaching. My Father will love him, and we will come to him and make our home with him.

—John 14:23

6
Somebody's
At Your Door

The four-year-old girl ran furiously up the stairs, tearing past her father in obvious rage. The startled daddy called out to her, "What's the matter, my sweet Princess?" Looking back at him with unabashed spitefulness, she stomped her tiny foot and shouted, "You're alive!" leaving the poor man reeling.

I have no idea what transpired between my friend and his little girl just after the unfolding of that awful scene. I'm quite sure the sweet fellowship of father and daughter was temporarily suspended. I can only imagine his hurt and think about what might have been. Had she run *to* her father rather than past him, fallen into his affectionate embrace and poured out her seemingly monstrous childhood troubles, how comforted she might have been, how cherished and indulged, how wisely guided and restrained.

But no. She would have her anger in spite of the wound it inflicted on the one who loved her most; in spite of the self-inflicted pain and loss it would cause. Had her dear daddy committed some egregious error that injured his child? Had his poor judgment harmed her in some way? Had he neglected her, been unkind or unfair to her?

Absolutely not. This friend of mine is the most conscientious and solicitous of earthly fathers. He was guilty of nothing but standing in the path of his furious child. He implored her to partake of his compassion and comfort, but she heartily refused.

Young women occasionally write to me revealing horrific pasts. Many of them have responded to Christ's sacrifice on their behalf, thereby entering into the family of God. They are forgiven, they know, and are thankful to have a new life and an opportunity to make for themselves and their families a home far different than any in which they have lived before. But there is a lingering problem, one that is a common theme in the communications I receive from women who were abused by their fathers.

"Please pray that I will find the loving Father-God that you have," one letter read.

"I have received Jesus as my Savior, but I'm still unable to trust God as my Father," wrote another woman.

"My father was a pastor and at the same time was abusing my two sisters and me. Because of this I still cannot bring myself to think of God as a father. Why do I need to?" asked another.

Is this a problem that you also share? If not, then you have something to be extraordinarily happy about. But you mustn't go running off in your bliss and neglect the things I'm about to tell you. There's an important message in this for you, too—one I hope you'll never forget.

If, on the other hand, this inability to see God as Father is your plight exactly, my heart is wrung out in sorrow for you. The concept of a father means fear and anguish and shame to you. Or perhaps it means rejection, forsakenness and pain. I know. I've been there.

Do you think perhaps you are responding to your earthly father's sin against you by running past your Heavenly Father's outstretched arms, refusing His eternally proffered presence and comfort? It would seem so to me. Do you imagine that by transferring the wickedness of your father onto God you will somehow find peace and justice? On the contrary, you will rob yourself of any hope of them in this life. Is that what you want? Of course not. You desire peace, love and comfort more than anything in the world, but you have spent your young life looking for them in all the wrong places.

Remember earlier when I spoke to you about focus? You turned your focus from your past to God. Now I want you to focus more sharply on Him. He has many attributes, many names. But just for now, don't think of Him as Savior, Messiah, Jehovah, Creator, Redeemer, Judge, Beginning or End. Not as Rock, Shepherd, Guide, Lion, Lamb, Refuge, Truth, Way, Spirit or Son of God. Yes, He is all of those and much more. But for now, He is Father. Let's take a look at why this is so vitally important.

If you are in Christ, God is already your Father. "Whoever acknowledges the Son has the Father also" (1 John 2:23). You can disobey Him. You can refuse to call him "Father." Still, He remains your Father and you His child.

Next, it is crucial that you come to grips with the fact that the connection you have made between your earthly father, who is a sinner, and your Heavenly Father, who is so pure that He cannot even look on sin, is invalid. For much, if not all, of your life you have been enslaved by fear because the father who should have protected and provided for you betrayed your trust. He proved himself to be unworthy of trust, so you were left unwilling to trust anyone at all. That is understandable and most unfortunate. It is also a fallacious concept vigorously encouraged by Satan, whose sole satisfaction (now that our souls are held securely out of his reach) is to procure misery for us through our remaining moments of mortality. He delights in seeing us run like ill-tempered four-year olds directly past the loving arms of our Father and into his own carefully woven net of suffering, self-pity and deception.

Are you going to keep on cooperating with that old serpent? You needn't do that. He's a liar and he was defeated 2,000 years ago by the Truth. The only control he has over your thoughts, opinions and ideas is that which you concede to him. Determine in your will that you are *not* going to believe his falsehoods about your Father anymore. Then ask God, through the power of the blood of Jesus Christ, to correct your thinking and to reveal Himself to you as your loving Father. And prepare yourself for a thunderous victory. It's a given. Thanks be to God! He gives us the victory through our Lord Jesus Christ (1 Cor. 15:57).

Finally, you must go directly to the words of our Lord Jesus and observe His explicit instruction to you concerning this matter. Is He satisfied for you to call God only by *His* name, Jesus, or did He come to reveal His Father to you that you might not be fatherless anymore? Let's take a look at the Gospel of John and then you decide:

"If you knew me, you would know my Father also" (8:19).

"My sheep listen to My voice; I know them, and they follow me. I give them eternal life, and they shall never perish; no one can snatch them out of my hand. My Father, who has given them to me, is greater than all; no one can snatch them out of my Father's hand. I and the Father are one" (10:27-30).

"Whatever I say is just what the Father has told me to say" (12:50).

"Whoever accepts me accepts the one who sent me" (13:20).

"No one comes to the Father except through me. If you really knew me, you would know my Father as well" (14:6-7).

"The world must learn that I love the Father and that I do exactly what my Father has commanded me" (14:31).

"The Father himself loves you because you have loved me" (16:27).

And don't forget Jesus' teaching concerning prayer: "This, then, is how you should pray: 'Our Father . . .'" (Matt. 6:9). Over and again we see Jesus praying thus: "Father . . . ," "righteous Father . . . ," "My Father . . . ," "*Abba*, Father . . . ," "Our Father . . . ." This was for your example, dear hurting Child. He knew this would be difficult for you, so He came, not to make a way to the Father for you, not to show you the way, but to be the Way to the Father. Jesus came to reconcile you to His *Abba* (Papa) Father so that He and His Father can keep company with you. "If anyone loves me, he will obey my teaching. My Father will love him, and we will come to him and make our home with him" (John 14:23).

God the Father wants to make His home with you! Think about that. He doesn't just want to visit with you now and then. He loves you much more than that. He wants to live with you for the rest of your life. And then He'll take you to live with Him forever!

Have you ever been inside a Victorian house? Even the simple farmhouses from that era, like the one I live in, had a front parlor where the lady of the house received visitors. The parlor was usually the most well-kept room of the house, outfitted with elaborate, if rather stiff, furnishings, and set apart for the distinct purpose of entertaining guests. Usually, family members, and especially children, did not enter the parlor for ordinary, day-to-day living.

It is interesting to note that extended family members, when visiting, were generally not given the "parlor treatment," but were free to roam the house at will in order to "keep company" with family members as they went about their daily activities. No uncomfortable horsehair upholstery for these guests! A front porch rocker or a wooden kitchen chair would do nicely as long as it meant being with cherished loved ones.

You're a cherished loved one too. Your Heavenly Father gave the richest treasure heaven could afford—His beloved Son—in order that He might "keep company" with you. He's knocking and knocking at your door, but not for the purpose of having a little visit in your parlor. He wants access to you, His cherished child, whatever you're doing, wherever you are. Believing this will open up a new world for you. If you're in the laundry room folding clothes, He'll be right there beside you. "Thank you, Father," you might say, "for these clothes you've provided for us." Washing dishes is much easier when there's Someone to talk to. "You're so good to us, Father, to so faithfully give us food to eat every day." When you're scrubbing the bathroom floor *again* and the children run in arguing *again*, you can look up quickly and cry, "Help me, Father! Give me wisdom and give me strength!"

You get the picture. But it doesn't work that way if God the Father is shut up in your parlor, or worse, hindered from entering your house altogether. Remember, He'll never barge in on you. He's a perfect gentleman. But look at Him standing there and so patiently knocking. And waiting. Oh, how He wants to come in!

As I was wondering what I could say to you to convince you of what a devoted, trustworthy Father He is, the words of a favorite hymn came to mind:

How firm a foundation, ye saints of the Lord,
Is laid for your faith in His excellent Word!
What more can He say than to you He hath said,
To you, who for refuge to Jesus have fled?

Of course, I thought. *He has already said everything that needs to be said. What on earth could I possibly add to "His excellent Word"?*

So I am privileged to deliver to you portions of the love letter He wrote to you long ago. Pay close attention to every promise of love, guidance and protection. Each of them is true, for "God is not a man, that He should lie" (Num. 23:19).

My dearly loved Child,

I have loved you with an everlasting love. I have drawn you with loving-kindness. You are the apple of My eye. I have inscribed you on the palms of My hands. No longer will they call you deserted . . . for I will rejoice over you. I will take great delight in you; I will quiet you with My love, and I will rejoice over you with singing. I will gather you into my arms and carry you close to my heart.

I do not willingly bring affliction or grief to the children of men. I thought you would call me "Father" and not turn away from following Me. For I know the thoughts and the plans I have for you . . . plans to prosper you and not to harm you, plans to give you hope and a future.

Come unto Me and I will give you rest. Take My yoke upon you and learn from Me, for I am gentle and humble in heart, and you will find rest for your souls. For My yoke is easy and My burden is light. My presence will go with you and I will give you rest. I am with you when you are with me. If you seek Me, I will be found by you. I go before you and will be with you; I will never, no never, no, never leave you or forsake you. Do not be afraid; do not be discouraged.

Look! I have been standing at the door and I am constantly knocking. If anyone hears Me calling him and opens the door, I will come in and fellowship with him and he with Me.

For I, the Lord your God, am a sun and shield; I bestow favor and honor. No good thing do I withhold from those who walk uprightly. If you remain in Me and My words remain in you, ask whatever you wish and it will be given you. Call upon Me in the day of trouble; I will deliver you and you will honor Me. I am the helper of the fatherless. I will deal with all who oppressed you. I am close to the brokenhearted and save those who are crushed in spirit. Before you call I will answer; while you are yet speaking, I will hear. Call to Me and I will answer you and tell you great and unsearchable things you do not know. Though you are surrounded by troubles, I will bring you safely through them. I will clench My fist against your angry enemies.

Let me have all your worries and cares, for I am always thinking about you and watching everything that concerns you. Indeed, the very hairs of your head are numbered. Fear not, for I am with you. Do not be dismayed; I am your God. I will strengthen you; I will help you; I will uphold you with my victorious right hand. Now you don't need to be afraid of the dark anymore, nor fear the dangers of the day; nor dread the plagues of darkness, nor disasters in the morning. Don't be afraid, for I have ransomed you; I have called you by name; you are mine. When you go through deep waters and great trouble, I will be with you. When you go through rivers of difficulty, you will not drown! When you walk through the fire of oppression, you will not be burned up—the flames will not consume you. For I am the Lord your God, your Savior, the holy One of Israel. The mountains may depart and the hills disappear, but My kindness shall not leave you. My promise of peace for you will never be broken.

If your father and your mother should forsake you, I, the Lord, will take you up. I will not leave you as an orphan; I will come to you. Can a mother forget her little child and not have love for her own *son? Yet even if that should be, I will not forget you. I am the Father of compassion and the God of all comfort. No mere man has ever seen, heard or even imagined what wonderful things I have ready for those who love Me.*

Now you are no longer a stranger to Me and a foreigner to heaven, but you are a member of My very own family, a citizen of My country, and you belong in My household with every other Christian. And so you should not be like a cringing, fearful slave, but you should behave like My very own child, adopted into the bosom of My family and calling to Me, "Abba, Father." For My Holy Spirit speaks to you deep in your heart and tells you that you really are My child. And since you are My child, you will share My treasures—for all I give to My Son, Jesus, is now yours too.

He who overcomes will inherit all of this and I will be his God, and he will be My son.

With My unfailing love,
Your Father

Do you hear Him now? He is constantly knocking. Have you ever witnessed such patience, such paternal tenderness? But the next move is yours. How will you respond to His loving promise, "If anyone hears my voice and opens the door, I will come in and eat with him and he with me" (Rev. 3:20)? You know this is what you've always wanted: to keep company with your immeasurably good and loving Father! You long to overcome your image as a pitiful victim whose "inner child" is never satisfied. You don't have to go on that way. You are a child of God. You can choose to embrace that lovely role right now if you will.

A letter I received this week contains this heart-wrenching statement: "I want so badly to sink into those everlasting arms and be held and loved with a daddy's love. My heart cries out for a mom and a dad." My response to that dear woman and to you, my Friend, is this: The everlasting arms are open wide. The Daddy's love is there from everlasting to everlasting. So what in the world are you waiting for? Get up out of your slough of distrust and go open that door!

More secure is no one ever
Than the loved ones of the Savior—
Not yon star on high abiding
Nor the bird in home nest hiding.

God His own doth tend and nourish,
In His holy courts they flourish;
Like a father kind He spares them,
In His loving arms He bears them.

Neither life nor death can ever
From the Lord His children sever,
For His love and deep compassion
Comforts them in tribulation.

What He takes or what He gives us
Shows the Father's love so precious
We may trust His purpose wholly—
'Tis His children's welfare solely

— Lina Sandell Berg

None of us is less or more worthy than the rest of us. We are all unworthy as we can be. That is why Jesus had to die.

7

Poor, Pitiful
Palace Dweller

Could you ever have dreamed it? There you were in that horrible pit with no hope of escape, and then along came the great God of the universe, who heard your cry and lifted you up, seating you in heavenly places, becoming your Father and making His home with you!

Now, because of that incredible grace He extended to you, you have set about creating a "heavenly home" for your loved ones, and everything is coming together like a fairy tale—except for one tiny hitch. You suffer terribly from that low self-esteem you've been lugging around all of your adult life. You hardly even know you have it, but people are always pointing it out to you. Some have even tried to encourage you out of it by telling you how special you are to them and to God and how you have no reason to feel that way about yourself.

That hasn't helped, though. As a matter of fact, the more aware of your poor self-image you become, the more entrenched you are in it. With the huge burden of unworthiness you are carrying around, it would be unfair to expect anything else of you. Did I say unfair? Why, it would be right down heartless and cruel!

Well, call me heartless if you must, but I *do* expect more from you because I care for you, and because I know God expects more too. We don't want to disappoint Him do we? He's the

One who lifted us out of the horrible pit. So what are you doing climbing back down into that slimy hole? You must perceive, either consciously or unconsciously, that there is some advantage in doing so. We'll come back to that later.

You have undoubtedly been told that you will never experience complete healing until you improve your self-image. That is a common theme among therapists and counselors today, even Christian counselors. I have searched the Scriptures for some basis or even a hint of this concept, but I haven't found it. I don't imagine to have wrung out in my finite mind all of the meanings and intentions of God's Word. But nowhere do I see any indication that men and women of Bible times were ever preoccupied with "finding themselves" or with their self-esteem. Nor do I see God promoting such preoccupation. God is truth, and truth has never been (nor will it ever be) a leader in the political correctness campaign. Truth is, in fact, an enemy of today's self-esteem revolution. Let me explain.

I have received numerous letters from women who struggle with "low self-esteem." Many, but certainly not all, have some form of abuse in their backgrounds. They usually write something of this nature: "My parents never accepted me or gave me unconditional love. They told me I was worthless. I could never measure up to their expectations. Now I'm a Christian with a family of my own and I have no self-esteem. I still feel worthless and unloved. Is there anything you can say that will help me?"

If that is where you are, my Daughter, and if that is what you are asking me, then yes, there is something I can say that will be of help to you. It's going to be painful, though, so if you think you're not up to that, you need to carry yourself and your poor self-image on to the next chapter and be done with this one right now. Not that I'm encouraging you to do that. I want with all of my heart for you to stay right here with me so we can go through this together. But I know that "no discipline seems pleasant at the time, but painful" (Heb. 12:11). Pain isn't the purpose of discipline though, is it? Of course not. It is simply the necessary means to a glorious end. "Later on, however, it produces a harvest of *righteousness* and *peace* for those who have been trained by it" (v. 11, emphasis mine).

Righteousness and peace—sounds wonderful, doesn't it? Then you must be willing to accept the sting of truth that produces it. It won't last long, I promise.

Why don't we begin by doing a comparison study? We'll compare or measure your self-image (what you think about yourself) with your true image (what God thinks about you). My guess is that you think you are unworthy and will never measure up. I hope this doesn't send you reeling, but you have just scored ten out of a possible ten points on the truth scale! You *are* unworthy and you *never will* measure up. But that is only part of the truth. The whole truth is this: You are unworthy, I am unworthy, and everybody who has ever drawn a breath, with the exception of Jesus the Messiah, is unworthy. He *alone* is worthy. Actually, you and I and everybody else are so hideously unworthy that we could never in a lifetime or in eternity fathom our unworthiness. Nor are we asked to do so. We're simply required to recognize that we're all in the same boat: "for all have sinned and fall short of the glory of God" (Rom. 3:23). This means that yours is not a special case. You're just like the rest of us, and we're all miserable, unworthy failures.

That didn't exactly buoy your spirits, did it? Well, this will, for there is still another facet to this great truth. You see, while it is true that you're unworthy and that just makes you one face in a crowd, it is also true that God doesn't see you that way anymore. That image of you was eternally washed away with the blood of Jesus Christ when you received Him as your Savior. We saw what Romans 3:23 said about our failure to measure up. Now let's look at verses 23 and 24 together: "for all have sinned and fall short of the glory of God, and are justified freely by His grace through the redemption that came through Christ Jesus."

You have been justified. That means God has declared you, a guilty sinner, righteous. This He has done *freely* by His grace, which is His undeserved favor. He redeemed you from your un-worthiness and now sees you in Christ, clothed in the right-eousness of Christ. But that redemption, free to you, cost God everything. He gave the treasure of heaven, His only begotten Son, to redeem your life from the pit. So you are of inexpress-ible worth to God.

When we realize that we are totally, hopelessly unworthy, it doesn't mean we have low self-esteem. It means we have a bib-lical view of ourselves. We *are* unworthy. None of us is less or more worthy than the rest of us. We are all unworthy as we can be. That is why Jesus had to die. My spiritual mother, Elisabeth Elliot, said it this way: "If you're OK and I'm OK, what was Jesus doing on that cross?"[1]

So our problem is not in seeing our failure to measure up. Understanding our unworthiness is what brings us to salvation. The problem is when, after receiving God's free gift of salvation, we remain focused on our unworthiness. God doesn't. He sees us in Christ and Christ in us and treats us like His own dear children, for that is who we are—accepted in the Beloved.

In spite of our position with God, obtained for us by His un-speakable mercy and grace, some of us go right on saying, "So-and-so treated me so badly all of my life that I can't help think-ing I'm a bad, unworthy person." Where is the logic in this? What difference does it make how you were treated? The King of Kings and Lord of Lords calls you His child. He's given you the keys to His palace. He entreats you to call Him "Father." He indulges you with His love. What more could He do to assure you of your worth? Whom will you believe—the eternal God, who by grace rescued you from the pit, or the people who helped hurl you into the pit to begin with?

"I don't want to believe them," you may be saying, "but how can I help it?" The same way you kept from dying in your sin. Put your faith in God's Word and what He has done for you. That's really all the Christian life is about. We choose to believe God or we choose to believe a lie. God has already told us all we need to know to be victorious in every aspect of our lives.

We simply don't believe Him. We think there must surely be something He's keeping from us, and when He reveals *that* thing we will have no trouble believing. Not so. That wouldn't be faith at all. God's Holy Word contains all of His revelation to us, and He has even said the faith to believe that Word will be given as a free gift. But gifts are never forced; they must be received. So what, or whom, is hindering you from believing what God says about who you are and what you possess in Christ?

There is one who would want you to believe a lie. The father of lies, old Lucifer, doesn't miss a trick. He knows that if he can keep your focus on your self-esteem (or lack thereof), then he prevents you from focusing on Christ. If you're focused inward, which is what the quest for self-esteem does, God can't very well use your life for His glory. If God can't use your life for His glory, that will reinforce your low self-esteem. It's a self-perpetuating lie. But you have the power to break free. It's called faith. Why don't you exercise it?

While we're on the subject of faith, let's take another look at Hebrews 11. We stopped there momentarily in a previous chapter as we were thinking about how the great men and women of the faith, who are held up for our example, obeyed God regardless of their emotions or feelings. Now let's look at another aspect of their stories.

The first thing that stands out in this inspiring passage is the phrase "by faith." It is recorded 20 times in this one chapter and is obviously God's commendation of the people whose names follow the phrase: Abel, Enoch, Noah, Abraham and Sarah, Isaac, Jacob, Joseph, Moses and his parents, Israel and Rahab. The writer of Hebrews goes on to say there just wasn't time to write about other heroes who "through faith" achieved a long list of victories for God's kingdom.

All of this makes for a wonderful study of faith, but what I want you to observe is the lack of any mention of how these children of God felt about themselves. We are told what happened to some of them, what God asked them to do and what they did. That is all.

Imagine a 20th-century spin on these stories. For the sake of time we'll just look at two of these greats of the faith, one man and one woman.

Picture, first, Noah on his therapist's couch. If anybody ever needed counseling, he certainly should.

"Tell me, Mr. Noah, what brings you to my office today?" asks the good doctor.

"I need help sorting through my feelings, sir," answers Noah, who is obviously in a depressed state. "I've been through a terrible crisis and I'm not feeling very good about myself."

"Go on," urges the counselor.

"It all started quite a long time ago. I really was a pretty good guy, doing what was right, walking with God. Come to think of it, I was the only friend He had at the time. He has a rather strange way of treating His friends, I can tell you.

"The next thing I knew, God was confiding in me a plan of enormous consequences and making me a partner in it. He actually told me—wait till you hear this—to build a box 450-feet long, 75-feet wide and 45-feet high, seal it with pitch so it wouldn't leak, and bring two of every sort of animal, bird and creeping thing into it along with my sons, daughters-in-law and wife! Try to imagine how immense a job that was! But it isn't the work that messed up my psyche. Oh, no. That was bad enough, mind you. It doesn't compare, though, to the mental abuse I endured."

"Mmm," hums the doctor. "Why don't you tell me about it."

"It was awful. Just awful. My wife was sure I'd been out in the sun too long. 'Build a gigantic ark and seal it for leaks!' she exclaimed. 'There isn't any water around here. People will think you're daffy. Think of our reputation, Noah. Think of your children!' You can guess how I felt after hearing that for a few years."

"No," replies the doctor, "tell me."

"I felt like a good-for-nothing husband and father, that's what," says Noah, dejectedly.

"Really?" the doctor responds. "Even though you were doing the right thing in obedience to God?"

"It didn't matter," Noah shakes his head for emphasis. "I only *walked* with God; I had to live with my wife."

"Go on."

"That wasn't the half of it. The epithets my neighbors hurled at me would curl your hair. They laughed at me and mocked me day after day after day. 'Rain!' they shrieked. 'And what on earth is rain? Where is this great flood? You're crazy, Noah. Nuts. A lunatic.' This went on for so long that I believe it. Nothing you say can change my mind. My self-esteem isn't low. It's gone, I tell you. Gone."

The counselor considers Noah objectively, then comments, "This is most interesting, Mr. Noah. If I understand the reports, you actually experienced quite a victory in the end with God saving you and your entire family while wiping your (and His) enemies off the face of the earth. Wasn't that some compensation for all you went through? I admit you had a rough time of it for many years, but God's blessing on all you did for Him, and the fact that the entire earth is inhabited with your descendents, must surely do something positive for your self-image."

Noah sighs dispiritedly, fidgets with his beard and finally answers, "What difference does any of that make? I endured the non-stop verbal abuse of those wicked people for almost a hundred years. You think I can just put it behind me and start over? Nope. I'm finished. Just an unworthy, useless, deranged old man. They said it for so long they convinced me. Victories aside, I'm a legendary flop."

Whew! Aren't you glad Noah's story is ancient rather than modern history? Here's what the Wonderful Counselor tells us about the saga: "It was through his faith that Noah, on receiving God's warning of impending disaster, with reverence constructed an ark to save his household. This action of faith condemned the unbelief of the rest of the world, and won for Noah the righteousness before God which follows such a faith" (Heb. 11:7, Phillips).

If Noah ended up with a self-esteem problem, at least we were spared of having to endure an account of it. Most likely nobody ever told Noah he *should* have a problem. Self-esteem just wasn't a hot topic back then. Oh, for the good old days.

Now let's think for a moment about Rahab. She was a prostitute in the land of Jericho who hid Joshua's spies in her house to aid him in taking the city as God had commanded him. She did this because she had believed on Joshua's God, as evidenced by her amazing proclamation of faith: "for the LORD your God is God in heaven above and on the earth below" (Josh. 2:11). Because she did this, by faith her life and the lives of her immediate family were spared, and she became the mother of Boaz, an ancestress of David and thus in the lineage of the Messiah. What a story! God can do anything, can't He?

But there is the problem with that one derogatory word that God used not once, but four times as He recorded Rahab's history. Rahab the *prostitute*. Now was that really necessary? After all, she was instrumental in helping Joshua carry out God's plan. Think how seeing her name in print with that little aside attached would have made her feel. If her story were played out today, I would imagine poor Rahab in a court of law, weeping before the judge.

"Oh, your Honor, I can't begin to express to you the pain and degradation I have experienced since the publication of that …that Book which contains the slanderous remarks about me. Why," here she weeps uncontrollably for about 30 seconds, then continues, "my self-esteem is so damaged that I'll be in counseling for years. That's why I must ask for a settlement of $26 million. Not that money could ever repay me for the personal pain and suffering I have endured, not to mention the destruction of my reputation. But at least it will be a small token to help me back on the road to mental and emotional healing."

Sounds pretty ridiculous, doesn't it? But anymore, a lawsuit against God could just be a matter of time.

Not in Rahab's day, though. All we know about her is what she did because of her faith and what God did for her in return.

Not one word, thankfully, about how her self-esteem fared through it all.

Had Noah and Rahab and the others been sitting around bewailing their poor self-images they wouldn't have accomplished anything for God. And they would have had what has become the classic excuse: "I can't do anything for God because I'm not worthy."

One more hard suggestion needs to be made before we leave this subject for good. I am aware that there truly are some individuals who have been so beaten down, so abused, so brutalized that they have absolutely no self-respect, no self-esteem, if you will. I know this is true because I've met a few of them. It isn't a pretty sight. These people, who I believe are few and far between, can certainly benefit from the assistance of a trained counselor.

Many, however, of the low self-esteem crowd have learned, perhaps quite subconsciously, that there is more than a little to be gained by being a part of that poor, pitiful group.

First, when one is constantly sighing about how worthless and useless she is, others who have even a minimal amount of compassion see the need to assure her otherwise. Even when this proves ineffective, the process continues because no one can think of anything else to do. Meanwhile, she begins to enjoy the attention and the constant affirmation, especially since she had to do nothing at all to earn it. Soon, feigning poor self-esteem is not out of the question because she has learned that a self-esteem problem is almost a magical tool of manipulation. After all, who's going to dump on a person who carries such an emotional burden around? Who's going to ask her to do her fair share? Who's not going to tiptoe around that one in order to avoid inflicting more damage on that already mutilated self-esteem?

Please, for the sake of Christ and your loved ones and yourself, forget about your self-esteem. Forget about your unworthiness. Forget about yourself. All of this self-absorption is nothing akin to the humility you are attempting to demonstrate. True humility is to think *nothing* of yourself. Anything else is actually an insidious form of pride. Release it—all of it—and turn your eyes upon our selfless Savior, who was God, yet "made Himself nothing" in order that it might be said: "Therefore, there is now no condemnation for those who are in Christ Jesus" (Rom. 8:1). I've been told that the original language in which that verse is written holds an even broader interpretation than the one we see in our less-colorful English. Yes, there is now no condemnation for us. But also there is now *no reason for failure* for those who are in Christ Jesus. No more excuses. Not even the awful way we have been treated, which resulted in our wretchedly low self-esteem.

The Word of God says of Jesus, "He humbled himself and became obedient to death—even death on a cross!" (Phil 2:8). That is how He procured victory for us. That is how we emerge victorious too: by humbling ourselves and becoming obedient unto death. Death to self is the only cure for a self-esteem problem. What corpse ever worried about its self-image?

The apostle said it this way: "I died on the cross with Christ. And my present life is not that of the old 'I', but the living Christ within me. The bodily life I now live, I live believing in the Son of God who loved me and sacrificed Himself for me. I refuse to make nonsense of the grace of God!" (Gal. 2:20-21, Phillips).

Are you making nonsense of the grace of God? You are if you see yourself as poor and pitiful. You're an inhabitant of the palace of the King! Why not try behaving as such?

> Commit thou all thy griefs
> And ways into His hands,
> To His sure trust and tender care
> Who earth and heaven commands;
> Who points the clouds their course
> Whom wind and seas obey:
> He shall direct thy wand'ring feet,
> He shall prepare the way.

Thou on the Lord rely,
So safe shalt thou go on;
Fix on His work thy steadfast eye
So shall thy work be done.
No profit canst thou gain
By self-consuming care;
To Him commend thy cause, His ear
Attends the softest prayer.

— Charles Wesley

he world's peace consists in the absence of untoward circumstances; Christ's is altogether independent of circumstances, and consists in the state of the heart.

—F. B. Meyer[1]

8
Peace and Contentment

Did you know that discontentment cannot cohabitate with peace? If you doubt that, then enter a home where peace is the obvious rule, and you can be sure that those who abide there have learned the great lesson of contentment. On the other hand, anyone who is not satisfied with what she has will not be satisfied with what she obtains.

"But," you protest, "you don't know the condition of this dilapidated apartment (mobile home, house, townhouse) where I have to live. Nobody could be contented here! If only I had a nicer home, with better furniture and modern appliances in a safer neighborhood, *then* I'd be happy."

Would you, really? I doubt it, because contentment doesn't spring from favorable circumstances. Contentment is a choice and may coexist with even the most abysmal of circumstances.

Fanny Crosby, the beloved hymn writer blinded at six months of age by a physician's mistake, understood this principle at an early age. When nine years old she wrote these words:

Oh, what a happy child am I
Although I cannot see;
I am resolved that in this world
Contented I will be.
How many blessings I enjoy
That other people don't!

To weep and sigh because I'm blind,
I cannot nor I won't.

That is an eloquent picture of a contented heart. At the tender age of nine Fanny already had recognized that she *could* weep and sigh over being blind and, most likely, get away with it. She resolved, however, that she wouldn't. She knew contentment in the face of adversity, and out of her satisfied heart flowed some of the sweetest gospel songs known to the church.

It has been said, "Most of us can, if we choose, make this world either a palace or a prison."[2] Permit me to tell you about a friend of mine who made her world a prison because of discontentment.

Amy and Russ (not their real names) lived in a very old, run-down apartment building. Amy hated it; Russ lived with it. The rickety place needed much in the way of repairs, but most of all it needed someone to clean it and put it in order. Amy had no desire to put forth that kind of effort, however, because, she said, "No matter what I do it'll never look good. I'm just gonna wait until Russ buys me a decent home. Then I'll keep a perfect house."

Meanwhile, it seemed Amy had resolved to be perfectly miserable. After all, if you're going to live in a pig sty you might as well wallow in it.

Years passed. The couple had few friends, and the ones they did have dreaded an invitation to their cramped, filthy abode. Each visit revealed dirty dishes stacked higher than ever, a floor coated with grit and crud, every surface as sticky as fly paper, dirty laundry strewn throughout, stacks upon stacks of papers, newspapers, magazines, etc. Suffice it to say it was a stomach-turning mess. One always left there feeling the need for a hard scrubbing with lye soap and a good cheering up as well. Amy had created for herself a depressing prison and everyone who entered that place knew it.

Eventually, Russ scrimped and saved enough to buy Amy a sweet little house with new furniture, modern appliances, lots of storage space and a fireplace—Amy's dream come true. She was thrilled! Together, they hung pictures on the walls and planned color schemes. Amy conscientiously dusted, vacuumed every wisp of lint off the floor, kept the laundry done, washed dishes, straightened pillows and chair cushions. The place was immaculate—for a few weeks.

The new routine wore off quickly, for Amy had formed in herself the habits of discontentment and laziness. So when her circumstances changed, she simply moved from one prison to another, because it was Amy who needed to change, not her surroundings.

Now, a dozen years later, the "new" house looks every bit as dirty, cluttered and rundown as did the old apartment. Amy hates it; Russ lives with it. How sad.

Ralph Waldo Emerson said, "Discontent is the want of self-reliance; it is infirmity of will."[3] As long as we believe that our happiness depends on what our husbands or anyone else can do or buy for us, we will surely live out our lives in abject misery. After they have bought or done that thing on which our satisfaction rests, there will always be the next thing . . . and the next. Such is the unsatisfying quest for satisfaction. It cannot possibly work.

There must be, then, a resolve, a firmness of will, to simply be contented with the circumstances that are our present portion, not because they are pleasant or comfortable or at all what we would choose, but because they are *given* by our wise and loving Father. Does this mean that we are to do nothing to improve our situation? No. You must never confuse contentment with lethargy. I'm not suggesting that it is somehow wrong to hope, pray or strive for beneficial changes in our condition. That would be ridiculous. What I am trying to impress on your heart is that you must never hitch your contentment to the desired upgrade. You can and must be contented *now*, right where you are. Then, neither improvement nor declination can affect your peace. Genuine contentment is unassailable.

My friends Jim and Joy are a stark contrast to Russ and Amy. When my husband and I met them they were living in a 150-

year-old, massive brick farmhouse, which they rented for $50 a month. After our first visit we knew they were paying too much. The house had no heat. Windowpanes were broken out. Electrical wiring was grossly inadequate; upstairs the children did their homework by the light of one naked bulb that dangled in the hallway. The house was in such terrible shape structurally that a freezer the family had been given couldn't be installed because the floor wouldn't sustain its weight. Rent-free, this place would have been a rip-off.

Jim and Joy were involved in a ministry that paid next to nothing. As our friendship grew and we spent more and more time with them, we couldn't help noticing that these dear people did without many things that most of the folks we knew took for granted. They weren't naked and starving by any means, but their clothing by any standard was barely sufficient, and we know for a fact that they sometimes dined on popcorn for lunch or supper because it was all they had.

Sounds rather bleak, doesn't it? But it wasn't in the least bit bleak. We never met anyone before or since who demonstrated the unmitigated joy and contentment that we saw in this couple and in each of their seven children. Never once did I hear one of them utter a complaint about *anything*. They loved God with all of their hearts, cheerfully served Him every day, gave freely of all that they had and enthusiastically received with profuse thankfulness whatever He chose to provide. That old house may have been ugly, but it was also immaculate; what it lacked in amenities was made up for in neatness. Everyone worked hard; everyone laughed often. It was a wonder to behold. Imagine the impact that family made on David and me when we were just starting our family. They taught us the great lesson of contentment without ever speaking the word. We still marvel at the memory of them.

I'll never forget the day we learned that God had called them to a new ministry hundreds of miles away. While my heart broke at the thought of losing them, I cherished the hope that God would give them a better place to live, something wonderful—at least with central heat and intact windowpanes. When I

expressed that sentiment to them, Jim responded, "Any p
God gives us will be wonderful. This place certainly was. So
now we can pack up all of our wonderful memories and take
them with us, and they'll always be a part of us and each new
place wherever God leads."

And then I knew that Jim and Joy had never seen the old, dilapidated farmhouse the way we had seen it. Their contentment
had made it a mansion, a mansion they would possess wherever they went, whatever their circumstances; a mansion that
most earthly kings would view with envy.

In the 1800s a church leader named E. B. Pusey listed five
practical suggestions concerning the acquisition of contentment. Such wisdom they contain! Read them. Copy them.
Memorize them. *Practice* them.

If we wished to gain contentment, we might try such rules as
these:

> 1. Allow thyself to complain of nothing, not even of the
> weather.
>
> 2. Never picture thyself under any circumstances in which
> thou art not.
>
> 3. Never compare thine own lot with that of another.
>
> 4. Never allow thyself to dwell on the wish that this or that
> had been, or were, otherwise than it was, or is. God
> Almighty loves thee better and more wisely than thou dost
> thyself.
>
> 5. Never dwell on the morrow. Remember that it is God's,
> not thine. The heaviest part of sorrow often is to look for-
> ward to it. "The Lord will provide."[4]

As I study Pusey's rules for contentment, I'm amazed at how
applicable they are to every area of life. Our vulnerability to discontentment is certainly not restricted to our possessions (or
lack thereof). Our sinful hearts know no limits in devices to
keep us miserable and ungrateful. One person may be perfectly contented in her modest, little house with no thought of
needing any material goods whatsoever. At the same time she
may be secretly harboring a multitude of criticisms against her

husband, believing she would be happier had she married someone else.

Then again, it may be a person's work that makes her dissatisfied. "If only I could stay at home with my children," one woman sighs as she rushes out the door to her place of employment.

"If only I could get out of this house and away from the mindless little duties of caring for all of these children," sighs the stay-at-home mom.

It doesn't always have to be the overall call on one's life that causes the conflict with contentment, either. Sometimes it's the seemingly trivial details of daily life that rub us the wrong way or cut across the grain of our stubborn wills, arousing in us a sense of restlessness even in the midst of work we love. Just last week as I was writing a chapter for this book, the thought struck me that my refrigerator *desperately* needed cleaning. (Note that thought processes that disturb our peace often contain hyperbole; hence the adverb *desperately*. My refrigerator did need cleaning, but there was nothing desperate about it.) Thoughts followed concerning how far behind I am in all of my other work. Pretty soon I was contemplating how I couldn't possibly get everything done that needed to be done. *If only I could spend less time writing*, I thought, *then I could keep up with my housework the way I always did before.*

A few days later when I was finally in the process of cleaning out my refrigerator, I actually caught myself thinking, *If only I didn't have to do this, I could devote more time to my writing.*

So you see, I experienced no peace regardless of which task had me occupied, because I wasn't receiving the assignment of each hour as from a loving Father's hand. Instead, I broke Pusey's rules by picturing myself in different circumstances and dwelling on the wish that something (the type of work at hand) were different than it was.

What I had failed to do was ask God to clearly show me my assignment for those days. He never fails me when I trust Him to prioritize my work. He'll never fail you, either. His will for us is peace, contentment and security. "LORD, you have assigned me my portion and my cup; you have made my lot secure" (Ps. 16:5). Every aspect of our lives—the things we possess, the people with whom we live and interact, the work we must do, the abilities we own, our health, our intelligence, our looks, even the weather—is given to us by our gracious, all-knowing Father. Our peace and contentment are not determined by what He chooses to give, but by the attitude with which we choose to receive what He gives. What is given today may be far different from that which was given yesterday. Tomorrow, it may be different still. Yet our peace can and should remain constant.

The apostle Paul wrote clearly that this steady state of contentment must be learned. It does not come naturally; no one is born with a contented heart. (If you don't believe me, you've never lived with a squalling, red-faced infant or a foot-stomping, tantrum-throwing two-year-old.) In his letter to the Philippian church, Paul wrote, "For I have learned to be content whatever the circumstances. I know what it is to be in need, and I know what it is to have plenty. I have learned the secret of being content in any and every situation, . . . whether living in plenty or in want" (4:11-12). Twice Paul said he had *learned* contentment. He even called "being content in any and every situation" a "secret." But he immediately goes on to reveal the confidential matter to us in verse 13: "I can do everything through him who gives me strength."

It is Christ who enables us to learn and practice contentment, and what an example to us is He! Think of Him, the all-sufficient, Self-existent One, God-only wise, to whom all power was given; the sinless One who hung the earth on nothing, who stirs up the sea by His power, at whose rebuke the pillars of heaven tremble. He willingly stepped out of eternity into the restriction of time, becoming a tiny, helpless fetus in the womb of an impoverished teenager, traveling the birth canal and finding His first cradle in a filthy stable; living in obscurity with His human parents for 30 years; enduring ridicule and scoffing, being reviled; having no place to lay His head; suffering all manner of oppression and affliction; and finally, being sentenced to the humiliating, torturous death of a criminal. Yet he did not open His mouth. Not a murmur. Not a complaint. Only a humble life lived in the joyful spirit of perfect contentment: "Even so, Father; for so it seemed good in thy sight" (Luke 10:21, KJV).

Where, I wonder, did Jesus learn such acquiescence? Could it have been at the feet of His young mother, who, upon being visited by an angel and informed of events that would change her life forever, responded, "I am the Lord's servant. May it be to me as you have said" (Luke 1:38)?

What are our children learning at our feet: *to be content* with all that the Father has chosen for us, or to *contend* with God over the trifles we think we must have in order to be truly happy?

Paul wrote to Timothy, his dear son in the faith, powerful words of advice that I now pass on to you, my daughter in Christ: "But godliness with contentment is great gain. For we brought nothing into the world, and we can take nothing out of it. But if we have food and clothing, we will be content with that. . . . Command those who are rich in this present world not to be arrogant nor to put their hope in wealth, which is so uncertain, but to put their hope in God, who richly provides us with everything for our enjoyment" (1 Tim. 6:6-8, 17).

Resolve today to learn and to practice the contentment of which Paul spoke and which our Savior so perfectly demonstrated. You will be rewarded with peace in your home, and a reflection of your own contentment in the lives of your children. Your husband will be amazed, and the world—well, the world will delight to see what God can do with one uncomplaining woman.

> O Lord! my best desire fulfill,
> And help me to resign
> Life, health, and comfort to thy will,
> And make Thy pleasure mine.
> Thy favor, all my journey through,

Shall be my rich supply;
What else I want or think I do,
Let wisdom still deny.

> — William Cowper

Drop Thy still dews of quietness
Till all our strivings cease;
Take from our souls the strain and stress,
And let our ordered lives confess
The beauty of Thy peace.
—John Greenleaf Whittier

9
Peace and Order

Life today is full of strain and stress, isn't it? We face challenges and difficulties unheard of by the generations who've gone before, right?

John Greenleaf Whittier lived from 1807 to 1892, and he certainly seemed to comprehend a need for deliverance from stress. In the hymn "Dear Lord and Father of Mankind," he eloquently entreats God for quietness, simplicity, rest and order. Yet we would reflect on his era as one of comparatively great simplicity, short on stress. We would, of course, be wrong. Each generation has its own strife; every individual suffers his own stress. The entire world is looking for peace. Where will it be found? Whittier knew. The reflection of God's beautiful peace is seen in the "ordered lives" of His children—not only during the relatively peaceful times of our lives (what would that prove?), but in the busy, noisy, "I-only-have-one-nerve-left-and-you're-jumping-on it" times. The world must be shown, and who but God's people can do the showing?

That is precisely why the old argument "It's only what I am on the inside that counts" doesn't have the ring of truth. What you are on the inside is revealed by what you are on the outside. That which the world sees when it looks at you and your home and family is an enormous part of your testimony. The vast majority of the folks who cross your path will never know any more about you than what they can assess from outward appearances. How can we then fool ourselves into believing that it makes no difference how slovenly we are since we have such loving hearts and good intentions? What we are *is* of utmost importance to God, and what we are will be evident in what we do and the manner in which we do it. What other evidence is there?

I don't know anyone who believes there is something to be gained by living in a state of order-deprivation. Everyone seems to strive or at least long for some semblance of neatness and order, and why not? We are made in the image of God. The full meaning of all that "the image of God" entails is incomprehensible, of course. "A comprehended God is no god," it has been said. But even our simple minds can recognize many of the qualities inherent to God, and one that is indisputable is His orderliness. Get your Bible and read again the awesome story of creation in Genesis 1-2. Every act of God in creation moved away from chaos and was performed according to a plan. Methodical wisdom was the rule, not "random acts of kindness."

Now, take a deep, calming breath, open your eyes and take an objective look around the home you're creating for your family. Is there at least a reasonable amount of neatness and tidiness evident there? If not, do you have some sort of a plan to change the situation? May I spend the next few minutes encouraging you to develop one?

What's that you say? All you have is a one-room apartment with furniture made of orange crates, so what difference does it make if everything is in disarray? My dear Child! Order is not about what you have; it is what you do with what you have. Remember my unkempt friend Amy from chapter 8? Like her, you may have to make do with so little for only a short while, but you will always have to live with the attitudes and habits you form in yourself today. Don't fool yourself into thinking you would behave differently if your circumstances were different. Chances are excellent that you wouldn't.

Speaking of fooling ourselves, I have heard repeatedly over the last few years the argument that some people are just naturally neat and some people are born with a propensity toward messiness, and there's not much anyone can do about it. How convenient for the "messies" among us!

Certainly some people do seem to innately possess more organizational skills than others. We vary greatly from one another in *every* skill level. Still, there are reasonable standards of achievement to which we all strive, each striving harder where skills are lacking, and finding some ease where skills are greater. It is never acceptable to simply throw up one's hands and declare, "It would take too much effort for me to perform this or that task well, so I'm not going to bother with it." If the task is within the realm of your responsibility then you must exert whatever amount of effort it takes to do the job well. We would not accept the "I'm not strong in that particular area" argument from any teacher, pastor, physician, nurse, mechanic or contractor, so why do we, given our high and holy calling as wives, mothers and homemakers, try to use it?

The truth is, maintaining some level of order in a home requires a great deal of time and energy from anyone. It also saves a great deal of time and energy (more about that later). It is often initiative rather than inherent skill that makes the difference between a chaotic and a peaceful home. As Christians we are to be imitators of God, not followers of our own inclinations.

As Oswald Chambers observed, "Most of us develop our Christianity along the line of our temperament, not along the line of God. Impulse is a trait in natural life, but our Lord always ignores it, because it hinders the development of the life of a disciple. . . . Impulse has to be trained into intuition by discipline."[1]

Another excuse for the lack of order in the home goes like this: "I have *important* things to do, so keeping my house clean and neat is not high on my list of priorities." Oh, really? And God didn't have important things to do when He whipped up our perfectly synchronized universe? Aren't we glad He made order a top priority?

Of course you have important things to do. Who doesn't? And you can do them much more efficiently if you have established order. The adage "A place for everything and everything in its place" is as helpful today (perhaps more so) as when it was first spoken. Have you ever delayed the completion of a ten-minute task simply because you couldn't find something the job required (a pen, the checkbook, a bill, the car keys, etc.)? Weren't you robbed of your peace as well as your time? Were you frustrated? Stressed? Has it occurred to you that you could experience more success in accomplishing those high-priority duties if you were better organized? Of course it has. The real question looming before us is, can it be done? The answer is an unequivocal yes!

"For God is not the author of confusion but of peace. . . . Let all things be done decently and in order" (1 Cor. 14:33, 40, KJV). This revelation of the nature of God and His desire for order in the lives of His children is not given to make us uptight, persnickety prigs. Rather, it was written for our example and encouragement. Notice that *confusion* in verse 33 is presented as the converse to peace. They oppose each other, and God, our Father, is the author of only one of the two—peace. We can infer, then, that if we choose a disorderly, confused lifestyle, we relinquish peace. We're certainly not going to make such a foolish choice as that, so let's take a look at how we may choose peace instead.

A few paragraphs ago I asked you to observe your surroundings and make an assessment as to the order or disorder of things. The reason this is so necessary is that we simply don't "see" our everyday surroundings. We close our eyes to the clutter that has piled up here and there: magazines, mail, newspapers, books, toys, laundry, unfinished projects, etc. An immunity develops. We get so used to the mess that we don't notice it. So keep on looking. Don't exclude any areas either. Drawers, closets and under the beds count too. And how about the basement, attic and garage? The tool shed? Don't worry. I won't follow you around and peek. This is a private exercise I'm recommending so that you can face the truth about where you register on the order scale. The first step to improvement is always the recognition that improvement is needed. Hopefully, I've already persuaded you that improvement is desirable.

. Before proceeding further, I must apprize you of the fact that what I am saying in this chapter is directed toward the "average" woman who, like me, is struggling to balance the varied responsibilities of being a wife, mother, homemaker, church member, neighbor and friend and still maintain a well-ordered personal life and home. If there were an actual 1-10 neatness scale, with 1 representing a disorderly mess and 10 a high degree of order, most people reading this book would probably fall somewhere between 3 and 7. There are people, however, who would peg the scale at either end. If you are one of those, I need to address you first.

Perhaps you would be off the chart on the neatness end of things. You are so exacting and meticulous about your housekeeping that your family lives in morbid fear of any semblance of dirt or disorder. Your children jump in terror over a glass of spilled juice. Your husband cringes if a greasy finger print is traced to him. You are tense and exhausted from unnecessary scrubbing, washing, vacuuming and dusting. Everyone is totally miserable. Home has become a place from which to escape, and, to be sure, there is no peace.

This is compulsive behavior and not at all the degree of orderliness I'm promoting here. If you see yourself in this description, please don't go on reading this chapter. You don't need this discussion; you need a different kind of help. Perhaps while the rest of us examine our disheveled linen closets, you might want to take another look at chapter 3 and prayerfully examine what the cause may be for your overzealous cleaning compunction. And please, don't hesitate to ask for help in sorting through what may be a maize of memories and emotions. The One who has already washed you whiter than snow is ready to help you find the answers you need. He wants to bring an end to your agitated overactivity. He is the Prince of Peace. I pray that you will permit Him to give you rest.

You may, on the other hand, be one of the few who would register a -20 on our imaginary scale. Dust bunnies are the least of your troubles. It would take a shovel to make a path through your living room. You never throw anything away because you "might need it someday"—as if it ever could be found if you did. Laundry and clothes needing repair are stacked so high that most of them are long outgrown or out of style. You haven't seen your vacuum cleaner for months. The overflow of stuff in your house is almost a health and safety hazard and is most certainly a threat to domestic harmony and peace. But you're overwhelmed and have completely given up. The situation is impossible.

Not so. As F. B. Meyer said, "You never test the resources of God until you attempt the impossible."² Elisabeth Elliot often says, "It is always possible to do the will of God." If you are ready to rely on the resources of your Heavenly Father, you can win over this mess. Do not despair. He wants your victory far more than you do.

Creating and living in squalor is just as much a compulsive behavior as is forcing yourself and your family to live in a state of hypercleanliness. But God will help you if you ask Him, and He knows just the people to bring across your path to assist you in sorting through your emotional baggage *and* to help plough through your domestic conundrums. I've already asked God to do that for you, my Daughter. Have you? "You do not have, because you do not ask God" (James 4:2).

Before I offer a few suggestions of my own on the subject of establishing order in the home, I want to recommend three books and a video that will provide a wealth of inspiration and practical help. First, *The Shaping of a Christian Family*, by Elisabeth Elliot, is the awe-inspiring story of the well-ordered home in which she and her five siblings grew up. You'll read in wonder as she relates how her mother and father maintained discipline, peace and order while at the same time providing plenty of love, laughter and happy memories for their four sons and two daughters. This isn't a how-to book but a candid account of how one couple did it, with fabulous results.

Elisabeth's video, *A Peaceful Home,* is also a treasury of helpful suggestions for achieving the family life of your dreams. It is one of the best resources available on the subject.

Two books by Donna Otto are must-read how-to books for every struggling wife and mother. Whether you're just starting out, you've got a few years of experience but could use a little organizational help, or you've made a seemingly disastrous mess of things, these books are for you: *The Stay at Home Mom,* which covers just about every area of home life, including orderliness, and *Get More Done in Less Time,* which offers step-by-step help in getting your home organized and keeping it that way.

Don't think for a moment that these resources are designed to put you in a straitjacket. On the contrary, they will encourage, inform and propel you into the freedom you now think is impossible to obtain. So run to the nearest Christian bookstore or to a church's lending library or to a friend who owns them and get started reading and changing your disorderly life forever.

One of Donna's profoundly helpful premises is this: "It isn't the things you do that make you tired; it's the things left undone." Think about it. Do you see how that has been true in your life? It certainly is in mine. When I finally force myself to face that long-procrastinated job (remember my "desperate" refrigerator?), I feel energized rather than tired. But the entire time I'm guiltily avoiding the chore, it nags me half to death. We're all pretty much the same in that respect, I venture. So why do we put off so many things? For more reasons than we could possibly discuss here, I'm sure. We'll look at just seven of them.

1. Plain, old-fashioned laziness.
2. Plain, old-fashioned procrastination.

These two are self-explanatory. I'm sure they could never apply to you. They must be included, however, for my *other* readers.

3. Fancy, newfangled busyness.

Let's stop and talk about this one for a moment. We women today really are busy. While we may enjoy innumerable conveniences unheard of by women in previous generations, we have responsibilities unheard of by them too. (Who taxied all those little Victorian children to their soccer games, anyway?)

Now, a woman is expected to play roles in school and church that take significant amounts of time and energy. Her children, in order to keep up with all other children, of course, *must* play sports and take every kind of instrument, dance, voice or theatrical lesson under the sun; and mom (who else?) certainly must chauffeur them. In addition, many more women work outside of the home or operate a business within the home than did so just a generation ago.

In light of this, how can anyone expect a woman who spends from 8 to 16 hours a day away from home to have time or energy for anything more than barely keeping life and limb together? No thinking person *could* expect more. That is why there must be an assessment made concerning priorities. Do your children really need all those extra-curricular activities? Wouldn't it be better to have them focus on one thing at a time instead of having the entire family juggling mealtimes, passing one another on the run (if at all) and living in a state of chaos? Ask God to help you decide where to draw the line on this frantically paced lifestyle. "If any of you lacks wisdom, he should ask God, who gives generously to all without finding fault, and it will be given to him" (James 1:5).

How about that job you're holding down away from home? Is your family truly in need of what money you manage to clear after child-care, transportation and clothing expenses, plus taxes? It very well may be that your family couldn't survive without your income. I'm only asking that you consider the possibilities. If you're a single mom or your husband insists you go to work for whatever reason, you owe an explanation to no one. God knows and will strengthen you for *all* of the work you have to do. We are often overwhelmed by our circumstances. He never is. Rest in His unfailing love and ask Him for the peace you so desire. He who ordered the stars into place and knows them all by name can bring order to your home as well.

Sometimes young couples try to accumulate in the first few years of marriage what their parents acquired through 25 years or more of hard work and sacrifice. Meanwhile, any pretense of peaceful family life and order in the home is lost in the shuffle. "Peace is better than a fortune," wrote Frances de Sales.[3] We would do well to believe that.

I am confident that God will give you wisdom and discernment as you consider the options He presents to you concerning your busy life. I know that you will place the overall welfare of your family above any self-interest or longing for material possessions, for in so doing you are spending your life for eternal purposes. It isn't likely that you will ever be applauded for it by this world, but He whom you serve will reward you.

Now, back to my list of reasons for why we put off putting our homes in order.

4. Undeniable softness.

Generations of women who've gone before us learned self-discipline and perseverance through all manner of hardship and were not indulged to believe that they only needed to do those things they liked doing. They would have hooted at such a notion. Rather, they learned to love doing those things that had to be done. How it would change the manner in which we work if only we would put that wise understanding into practice!

For order to be achieved in a home there are legions of mundane jobs that must be performed *repeatedly*. There is no getting around it. The oven must be cleaned. The floors must be swept and scrubbed, the carpets vacuumed, the furniture dusted. Beds need to be made. Laundry must be done. Cabinets and closets should be straightened. Sinks, showers and tubs must be cleaned. Groceries have to be purchased and put away. Meals must be prepared. Whew!

Then there's motherhood: diapers to be changed, noses wiped, boo-boos kissed. There are stories to read and doctors to visit. Sick children need rocking. Children with nightmares need comforting. School children need transporting. Misbehaving children need disciplining.

Let's face it. No one really loves to do all of those tasks. Some of them are mindless, some exacting, most are tiring; but all have to be done. Putting them off or doing them begrudgingly keeps us in a state of unrest and constant dissatisfaction. It also teaches our children to shirk unpleasant responsibilities. They are all too willing to learn from us that a distasteful job can be performed in a slipshod manner, if at all. "The path to the self-disciplined child is the path forged by the self-disciplined adult," said Peter Haiman. There are no shortcuts in child rearing. Your children may not hear a thing you say, but they never fail to observe and imitate the things you do.

With that understood, why not, for the sake of your children and yourself, take a different approach? Do your least favorite tasks *first* and resist the urge to grumble about them. Why not make the best of it? Put on a favorite tape or CD and sing along while you spend an afternoon cleaning, sorting clothes or straightening a closet. (I love Christmas music. I start listening to it in October—I'd start sooner but my husband can't bear it—and it lightens my heart for any task.) Listen to a book on tape while you tackle a dreaded chore. Sing along with the radio. Hum a hymn. Whistle. You'll be amazed how much more quickly and easily your tasks will be accomplished when you confront your work with a merry heart. And when the job is completed, you'll really have something to be merry about. Then go back to your mental or written "to do" list, scratch off what's been done and tackle the next chore, and so on. The relief you'll experience by getting those distasteful jobs out of the way will more than repay you for energy expended.

Perhaps you're wondering, *Why bother with all of this organization and neatness stuff? No one appreciates a thing I do. No one even notices.* Most women feel that way at some time or another. Husbands and children rarely have any idea of all the roles a woman plays in the home. As Elisabeth Elliot has said, "The work you do as a mother and wife is generally not noticed as long as you do it. It certainly will be noticed if you don't do it. And that's true of all servants."[4] The real key to finding joy in this apparent injustice is in realizing whom it is that you serve. Of course you're serving your husband and children, but in so doing you've become the handmaid of the King! "Whatever you do, work at it with all your heart, as working for the Lord, not for men, since you know that you will receive an inheritance from the Lord as a reward. It is the Lord Christ you are serving" (Col. 3:23-24). Could that possibly apply to humble housework? I believe it *especially* applies to what we would consider humble work. God knows that our hearts tend toward ease. So He encourages us in the necessary discipline of mundane tasks by reassuring us of the importance to Him of all that we do.

Did you ever consider, when you are laundering your husband's grimy work clothes, folding all those tiny baby socks, cleaning around the edges of the bathroom floor or sitting up all night with a sick child, that you are serving God just as gloriously as if you were on foreign soil winning souls? If you faithfully do the work He has given you to do, not asking, "What am I, the maid?" but exclaiming in your heart, "Behold, the maidservant of the Lord!" then it is so. God's choicest servants have always understood this principle.

Listen to a few of them:

If God gives us but little tasks, let us be content to do little. It is pride and self-will which says: "Give me something great to do; I should enjoy that; but why make me sweep the dust?"— Charles Kingsley[5]

If you are a mother, you don't need to worry about looking elsewhere for service for God. Motherhood is your service.— Elisabeth Elliot[6]

There are strange ways of serving God;
You sweep a room or turn a sod,
And suddenly to your surprise,
You hear the whirr of seraphim,
And find you're under God's own eyes
And building palaces for Him.
— Herman Hagedorn[7]

Towels and dishes and sandals, all the ordinary sordid things of our lives, reveal more quickly than anything what we are made of. It takes God Almighty Incarnate in us to do the meanest duty as it ought to be done.
— Oswald Chambers[8]

If by doing some work which the undiscerning consider "not spiritual work" I can best help others, and I inwardly rebel, thinking it is the spiritual for which I crave, when in truth it is the interesting and exciting, then I know nothing of Calvary love. —Amy Carmichael[9]

Bringing order to a household can seem like thankless, discouraging work. Perhaps knowing that you are in the King's employ will bring an infusion of energy to your labors. God never promises to make things easy. Jesus said, "If anyone would come after me, he must deny himself and take up his cross daily and follow me" (Luke 9:23). Have you learned to deny yourself? It's a requirement if you're to be a disciple of Christ, and now is as good a time as any. Which job is it that you've been putting off the longest because you despise doing it and there are so many other things you'd rather be doing? Why not go ahead and start that job today? Lay aside this book and all the reasons why you couldn't possibly begin that job now. Of course you can. Just get up and do it.

Now let's see if we can turn up another underlying cause for a chronically chaotic house.

5. Failure to manage time.

While beauty and riches are divided unequally, every woman is allotted the same number of hours in her day. It's true that some women have more responsibilities to fill that allotment than do others, but I've observed that it's usually those very busy women who are the most dependable at getting extra projects done. Why? Because they rarely waste any time.

Napoleon said, "The reason I beat the Austrians is they did not know the value of five minutes." While you may not be engaged in actual warfare, you still have much to gain by learning from the Austrians' mistake. "Dost thou love life?" asked Benjamin Franklin. "Then do not squander time, for that is the stuff life is made of."

At a conference where I was speaking, a woman confided in me that her house was far worse than disorderly, and that she had been unable to get control of the situation no matter how hard she tried. She didn't work outside of the home, she told me, and she had only one child who was of school age, so he was gone most of the day.

This information piqued my curiosity, so I inquired about a few more details of her life. No interesting clues turned up until I asked this crucial question: "What time do you get out of bed in the morning?"

"Oh, I'm always up by eleven," she said.

I attempted to hide my shock.

She added (in response to my bulging eyes, no doubt), "I've never been a morning person."

I must respond to that statement just the same as I responded to the "domestically impaired" individual's lament: How convenient! So, all we have to say is "I'm a _____," or "I'm not a _____ ," and we're relieved of many of the reasonable responsibilities of life?

What a jester you are. You really had me going there for a minute. Of course you know better than that. Morning happens. Housework happens. We're adults now. We have to cope.

My advice to that bedraggled woman was the same advice I give to you, my Daughter: If you're really so tired that you can't roll out of bed much before noon, you need to have a checkup to make sure there isn't anything physically wrong with you. When physical problems have been ruled out, I would strongly suggest that you begin setting your alarm clock to get you up 15 minutes earlier for a few days. Then back it up again and again until you're getting up early enough to reclaim your day. You'll most likely need to get into bed a bit earlier at night, too, and all of this must be done by degrees. As Mark Twain said, "A habit cannot be tossed out the window; it must be coaxed down the stairs a step at a time."[10] Set a target time that you think is achievable and work toward that goal. You'll be amazed at how energized you'll feel just by bringing about such a positive change in your life.

When you do manage to get up, do two things right away: make your bed (assuming your husband isn't still in it) and get yourself dressed. This gets you moving in the right direction and prevents the blahs that develop from lounging around in your bathrobe.

Learn to plan ahead and set goals for each day. This doesn't have to be a rigid schedule; just a basic guideline of what you would like to accomplish. And make your goals realistic. You don't want to discourage yourself by being overzealous, nor do you want to grossly underestimate what you are capable of doing.

Watch out for time stealers such as TV and the telephone. Remember the poor Austrians! Five minutes will become 60 without your even thinking about it. And don't forget what Mr. Franklin said, either. It isn't just time you're wasting—it's your life. Don't let something so infinitely precious slip right through your fingers while you're watching a sitcom rerun for the umpteenth time.

Before I leave the subject of time management, I must tell you that the most important thing for you to accomplish each day is time alone with God. This is when you spend quiet time in His Word, receiving guidance and light for that day. You spend time talking to Him, too, casting your cares on Him, thanking Him for blessings received, asking Him to meet every need of your heart, offering your day's work to Him as a sacrifice. This is the most critical hour of your day. Don't ever think of skipping it to save time. Time with God *is* saved time. Apart from God you can do nothing. "In quietness and trust is your strength" (Isa. 30:15).

6. Failure to manage stuff.

Donna Otto has a wonderful formula for getting control of clutter. It works for cleaning out a single drawer or for shaping up an entire house. Here it is: put away, give away or throw away. Sounds simple, doesn't it? And it is simple unless you're in some kind of bondage to material possessions ("stuff"). Then you can't part with anything, so everything is in your "put away" pile (which is inching toward the ceiling). Of course, there's no place to put away that much stuff, so that results in a house, garage, attic and basement full of clutter.

This problem doesn't take care of itself. It only increases with every passing day. You must decide to do something about it. Just making up your mind to take action will propel you toward success.

Then you must get quite serious about giving away and throwing away. You probably have many useful items such as gadgets and clothing that you no longer use but that someone else could. My spiritual mother says she gives away anything in her closet that she has not worn for an entire year. You may want to give it two years, but certainly no longer than that. You aren't using it; someone else needs it. Giving it away will open up more space for your "put-aways."

Throw-aways are the junk you've been stashing—broken things, ruined clothes, worn-out shoes, old newspapers—unusable items that somehow never made it to the trash pile. They're begging you to take them; I'm begging you to take them. Today!

By the way, as you gradually change your image from pack rat to "throw-away maniac" (my children have called me such a name), you will gain the added benefit of others' neatness. You see, they won't leave any of their junk lying around in your path, lest you exercise your new clutter filing system on their behalf. It's magical.

Now all you have left are your absolutely necessary, can't-live-without-'em put-aways. After getting rid of all your old unused stuff and junk, you should have a great deal more drawer, closet and other storage space. Find a storage system that works for you and use it. In *Get More Done in Less Time*, Donna Otto offers many helpful ideas on how to set up a storage system of boxes that will keep your possessions organized and easy to find.

But ideas alone won't get the job done. Formulate a plan. Make some difficult choices. Then spring into action.

My older daughter went early one morning to baby-sit one of her favorite charges. She rang the bell and soon the door was swung open by the precocious three-year-old girl, who, with widening brown eyes and hands firmly placed on her tiny hips, proclaimed, "Come on in, Charlotte." There was a long sigh. "Mama's not ready yet. She just can't get her mess together."

What I'm telling you, as plainly and as politely as I know how, is this: "Get your mess together!"

7. Confusion about roles and authority.

Young mothers often err in the training of their children because they love them so much that they are terrified of repeating the mistakes made by their parents. This seems to be particularly true of women who were unloved, rejected or abused as children. They are determined that their child will never be made to feel as they did, and so they go about unintentionally setting up a situation that will lend itself to abuse. Please permit me to explain.

It is widely known that children are messy creatures by nature. (What else are strained peas good for if not finger painting?) They are famous for creating havoc in even the most orderly of homes. Part of their infamy is earned, I would concede, but part of it is brought about by a lack of understanding of at least four simple facts that were taken for granted a few generations ago:

◆ Loving discipline is not abuse; absence of discipline is abuse.

♦ Mothers are not required to be their child's full-time play-mate.

♦ Children are not made secure by nor do they have any need for a horde of expensive toys.

♦ Children are perfectly capable of helping with all sorts of housework at a very early age.

Since the primary focus of this book is not child rearing, I will touch on this subject only briefly. Again, I would recommend *The Shaping of a Christian Family*, by Elisabeth Elliot, for a more in-depth look at the way her mother went about raising children for God. Also, *Hints on Child Training*, written more than 100 years ago by H. Clay Trumbull (Elisabeth's great-grandfather) and recently reprinted, is a remarkably clear and helpful guide on the subject.

If there are children in your home, you already have an idea of how child training fits into a chapter on peace and order. If you're still waiting for children, it can't hurt to learn a few things ahead of time. If your children are almost grown, it's never too late to change direction if need be. Children need to see that parents are still learning too.

Much of what I'm about to say is my opinion. Some of it I learned through the experience of raising four children; some by listening to and observing other parents. These are things I wish someone had told me when I was just starting out as a mother. Prayerfully, I pass them on to you.

All good mothers, and especially those who were abused as children, fear ever approaching anything akin to abuse of their own children. That is reasonable and appropriate. We should have a healthy fear of crossing that line.

The trouble is, some women confuse *all* correction and discipline with abuse. That thinking is unbiblical and thus harmful. Children who are not given reasonable limits for their behavior—boundaries, if you will—are the most insecure children. And why not? The Bible says they aren't loved by their parents (Prov. 13:24). And I can assure you that they aren't loved by other people. No one wants his home invaded by unruly savages. A child who is not trained to understand the meaning of "no," "don't touch" or "come" won't be a welcome guest even in the home of Mommy's best friend. Nor will he contribute much peace and order to his own home.

An average child can understand and be expected to obey simple commands such as "no" by the age of 12 months and certainly by 18 months. If you do not train the child to respond with obedience at that young age, it will be no time at all before he can understand much more complicated requests, such as "You know perfectly well you aren't supposed to play Tarzan on the crystal chandelier. Get down from there this instant!" You'll probably find yourself saying it, too, with less-than-outstanding results.

If you're the mother of an adorable 18-month-old and you simply cannot bring yourself to spank his chubby little hand when he clearly understood your "no" and defied you anyway, then you need more assistance than I can give you here. *Please*, look for an older woman in the church or neighborhood whose children turned out reasonably well and ask her to mentor you. I'm praying that our Father will send just the right one to help you.

Meanwhile, turn to the Word of your Father. You know He will never deceive you or lead you astray. He loves your little one far more perfectly than you do, yet He admonishes you, "Discipline your son in his early years while there is hope. If you don't you will ruin his life" (Prov. 19:18, Living Bible).

In addition to being afraid to correct children, young mothers today seem to have the idea that it is their duty to play with their children all day long, or at least shuttle them all over town from parks to play groups. This is done for the purpose of "socializing" them. (Have they not recognized that God aptly planned for the socialization of children? That is why He put them in *families*.) Is it any wonder, then, that there is no time left for keeping order in the home?

I'm not saying that you are to stay so busy with housework that you can't ever play with your children. You most certainly can and should play with them. But there is work to be done, and the message we want to impart to them is that work comes first, then play. Remember, our children learn this by what we do rather than by what we say.

Mothers of yesteryear seemed to grasp another important facet of this same jewel: instead of a child commanding center stage of the parents' universe, the parents were the center of the child's universe. Parents were in charge; children weren't. This arrangement fit into the mother's workday quite nicely. I heartily endorse the idea.

When my children were small they loved following me around as I did my work. Sometimes they helped me (more about that later); sometimes they played with each other in the room where I was busy or sat nearby with a toy or book. I was always watching and listening and was available to answer questions or meet their needs. I was not, however, constantly playing with or entertaining them. They certainly didn't seem to think they were missing out on anything, and I rarely had any difficulty getting through the work I had planned for the day.

Sometimes loving mothers who were unloved themselves as children smother their own children with intense affection and indulge them with innumerable costly toys, thinking this is necessary to prove to them that they are loved. Don't believe it.

Please listen to reason. If it were necessary to give your children expensive things to make them feel loved, children from poor families would never feel loved, would they? And we both know that isn't the case. Love cannot be purchased; honest, selfless love does not manipulate. Your child already adores you. Just relax and revel in it.

As I look back now, my children probably had too many purchased playthings. Even so, it was usually simple household items such as pots and pans, nesting measuring cups, cardboard boxes and spools of thread that kept their attention the longest. My 18-year-old daughter, Sarah, recalls as her fondest memory sitting on the floor of my sewing room as I stitched her new clothes, playing with the dozens of brightly colored buttons from my button box. We spent many happy afternoons that way—I, accomplishing a needful task, and she, keeping herself entertained creating endless games with an inexpensive collection of buttons. Think of the money I could have saved! Why don't you learn from my mistake? Just a few carefully selected toys will more than suffice. And there'll be fewer things to pick up when you and your children tidy up at the end of a long day.

Speaking of picking up toys and such, I'd like to conclude with a thought we brushed past earlier. Do you realize that even your very young children are capable of helping you around the house? It's true. No one told me this when my first two children were small, and I somehow developed the idea that it was my job to wait on them hand and foot. That seemed like the nurturing thing to do. Fortunately, God gave me a spiritual mother before my younger two children were much out of babyhood, and she taught me better.

Not only are young children capable of helping, but they are amazingly willing as well! Two- and three-year-olds can fold washcloths, pick up and put away toys and carry unbreakable dishes to the sink. Four- and five-year-olds can dust, sort laundry, make their beds and wash dishes. School-age children can be responsible for their books, papers and homework assignments, vacuuming, folding laundry, cleaning sinks and tubs and helping to prepare meals.

You'll be amazed at how quickly your child masters new skills and how he beams with the satisfaction of a job well done. Your praise is meaningful because he truly is performing a valuable service. (Children always see through empty praise such as, "This is a fabulous drawing, Kara! What is it?") Meanwhile, your child is developing confidence and a work ethic and will understand what many children never learn: that play is always more enjoyable after a period of work. And you are gaining an able helper as you fight the good fight for an orderly, peaceful home.

Don't think of your children as a liability on the clean-home front. Sure, they're going to make messes, break things and fall far short of perfection many times when they help you. Still, they are your greatest asset and, when taught the discipline of conscientious work, will be an asset to their own families later on and to the kingdom of God as well.

Now that you are armed with this knowledge, I am confident that you will never permit laziness, procrastination or busyness to keep you from the noble work God has called you to do. Certainly you won't seek after softness, forget the value of five minutes or fail to get your mess together. You most definitely will cease underestimating your child's ability to help you serve the Lord Christ in your peaceful, orderly home.

I'm so proud of you that I think I'll have another cup of that delicious tea to celebrate! While I'm out in the kitchen filling our cups, why don't you meditate on this provocative thought?

The daily round of duty is full of probation and of discipline; it trains the will, heart, and conscience. We need not to be prophets or apostles. The commonest life may be full of perfection. The duties of home are a discipline for the ministries of heaven.— H. E. Manning

Better a dry crust with peace and quiet than a house full of feasting with strife.

—Proverbs 17:1

10
Peace and Quiet

Everyone seems to need it once in a while. Some people would give anything for a little of it. No one knows what to do about the present-day lack of it. I'm talking, of course, about peace and quiet.

Let's be perfectly still for a moment. Shhh. Just listen.

What do you hear? Even as we sit in attempted quietness there is the bombardment of real-life surround sound: children arguing, the TV blaring, a radio playing, the oven timer buzzing, dogs barking, wind chimes chiming, engines running, horns blasting, telephones ringing, Nintendos beeping, your baby crying and me trying to talk to you about peace and quiet. I SAID, "AND ME TRYING TO TALK TO YOU ABOUT PEACE AND QUIET!"

Sorry. I didn't mean to raise my voice, but it was obvious you couldn't hear me over all the clamor. What do you say we take some decisive steps toward a quieter environment so we can continue this brief but important conversation? I'll go and re-solve the toddler dispute, you see if you can get that sweet baby settled down, and on the way back we'll turn off all electronic devices. We'll have a ten-minute pandemonium moratorium. Agreed?

Well, that took a while but it was worth it. At least we can speak in a normal tone of voice and be heard. I'm feeling better already—and no wonder: the word *noise* comes from the French word *nois* (sound, din, uproar, quarrel), which originated from the Latin word *nausea*! Perhaps if we cease to think of our homes as being a bit noisy and instead begin to understand that they are actually *nauseating*, we will be better motivated to improve our auditory environment.

We have to face facts. There is plenty of noise over which we have little or no control: traffic sounds, neighborhood dogs barking, loud music next door, children squealing in the pool two doors down. Sometimes we can speak (quietly, of course) to the offending parties, and most communities have ordinances that can be invoked if a neighbor's noise becomes excessive and unbearable. But the truth is that life is loud, and we simply have to adjust.

Within our own homes, though, an effort can be made to lower life's volume. It will take an effort because old habits die hard. Why bother, then? Thanks for asking.

Above all, peace and quiet matters to God: He has much to say to us each day and He tends to speak in a "still, small voice." How will we hear Him if we are never quiet? It is difficult enough to concentrate on the visible and audible while being relentlessly buffeted by domestic sounds. How much harder is it, then, to focus on the inaudible message of our invisible Father? Yet His wisdom and guidance are the most important message we could possibly receive. Therefore, we must discipline ourselves to develop and maintain a quiet spirit, which God calls "incorruptible beauty" and which is very precious in His sight (1 Pet. 3:4, NKJV).

So how do we become quiet in spirit? For starters, by *being quiet* ourselves. Most of us do love to talk. I know I do. And our loving Father wants us to talk to Him, to tell Him all of our troubles and cares, to offer praise with our voices, to speak of Him in the great assembly, to talk to our children about Him all day long. But He also wants to talk to us. He desires our quietness. He is honored by our silence.

> Let all mortal flesh keep silence,
> And with fear and trembling stand;

Ponder nothing worldly-minded,
For with blessing in His hand
Christ our God to earth descendeth
Our full homage to demand.

      — Liturgy of St. James

Do you make time in your day to keep silence before Him? During that time (which can be only minutes, if necessary) do you strain to keep your focus totally fixed on your holy Lord, not permitting your thoughts to become "worldly-minded" or, if they do, bringing them back again and again to Him? If you faithfully work at this discipline—and it is amazingly strenuous work—God will begin to form in you that lovely, quiet spirit, which is of such great worth to Him.

In His infinite wisdom, God has commanded that we be still: "Be still before the LORD and wait patiently before Him" (Ps. 37:7). "Be still, and know that I am God" (Ps. 46:10). "Be still before the LORD, all mankind" (Zech. 2:13). In His incomprehensible mercy, He enables us to obey: "He makes me lie down in green pastures, he leads me beside quiet waters, he restores my soul. He guides me in the paths of righteousness for his name's sake" (Ps. 23:2-3).

Then, in His immense love, the Lord links our quietness to other attributes and blessings: "The fruit of righteousness will be peace; the effect of righteousness will be quietness and confidence forever" (Isa. 32:17). "In quietness and confidence shall be your strength" (Isa. 30:15, NKJV). "Make it your ambition to lead a quiet life, to mind your own business and to work with your hands, just as we told you, so that your daily life may win the respect of outsiders and so that you will not be dependent on anybody" (1 Thess. 4:11). "Therefore I exhort first of all that supplications, prayers, intercessions, and giving of thanks be made for all men, for kings and all who are in authority, that we may lead a quiet and peaceable life in all godliness and reverence" (1 Tim. 2:1-2, NKJV).

Enthralling, isn't it? Righteousness yields a crop of peace, quietness and confidence. Quietness and confidence yield strength. A quiet life garners respect and is a reflection of godliness and reverence. But before the harvest there must always be the toil of hoeing, planting, watering, weeding and fertilizing. In your quest for a quiet spirit and all its accompanying benefits, only you can do that work, for no one can be still before God on your behalf. The psalmist said, "*I* have stilled and quieted my soul; . . . like a weaned child is my soul within me" (Ps. 131:2, emphasis mine). As you exert the mighty effort it takes to be quiet before God, you will discover new depths to His love, and He will reveal Himself to you as He never could in the haste and hubbub of your otherwise hectic life. "Like a weaned child" you will rest in His paternal tenderness. The complexities of your life will not be as troublesome to you. Peace will begin to rule in your heart, and that is the first step to having peace rule in your home.

Henry Ward Beecher made this observation: "A mother's heart is a child's schoolroom." Every mother knows that is true, though it leaves all of us at times exclaiming, "Alas!" Who among us has not had the embarrassing experience of having the contents of our unpeaceful, disquieted hearts paraded before the world in the behavior and conversation of our offspring?

My friend Lynnette told me that her little girl, Logan, is always saying, "Mommy, I want to be just like you." This had already smitten Lynnette's heart with fear, but it didn't make its full impact until one morning when she overheard Logan fussing with her dolls in an all-too-recognizable tone of voice. "I have had it!" the four-year-old declared. "I'm not cleaning up this mess one more time!"

Our hearts *are* our children's schoolrooms. What are our precious little ones learning there? We will undoubtedly be shown if we listen to and observe them carefully. Children are like mirrors, reflecting our own images back to us, which is humbling and unnerving more often than not. But think of the potential for good if we, too, will be mirrors, reflecting the beautiful image of our Father! If only we will be still long enough to catch

His image, He will do the work of transforming us into that image, which is His overruling purpose for our lives. Then we become cooperators with Him in all that He wants to accomplish in and through us—everything from leaving our sordid pasts behind us right down to bringing peace and quiet to our homes. I cannot overstate the importance of the habitual, sacrificial act of stillness before God. You cannot practice quietness (or anything else for that matter) in your external life if it is not an internal reality. We must *become* quiet before we can expect to *behave* quietly.

Having understood that, we are ready to make visible what has already taken place in our spirits. The first step in the direction of positive change is usually evaluation. What causes most of the uproar in your home? Listen and think about it.

If your home is like most there is a high level of background noise, and you can become so accustomed to it that, like clutter, it goes unnoticed. Television is the primary source of noise pollution in the home. Not only is it noisy in and of itself, but it is a major purveyor of the world's message, which is the antithesis of peace and quiet. Certainly and at the very least, it should be turned off if no one is sitting down watching it. That would eliminate some unnecessary racket. You and your husband should sit down together and come up with a viewing plan for your entire family that limits the amount of time any of you sits in front of that mind-numbing tube. My husband and I did that 20 years ago, and we decided to just get rid of the TV. We haven't regretted it for a moment, and our children didn't make a fuss about it either. (Of course, they weren't born yet!)

Interestingly, our oldest child, Charlotte, who is in her first year of college, called home last week to get some statistics on American family television viewing. She's required to give a persuasive speech in her communications class, and she's chosen "The Ill Effects of TV on Family Life" as her topic. And we think our children aren't listening.

If you and your husband are not united on this subject (I've heard this complaint often from women who would love to get rid of or restrict the TV), please do not think of nagging him over it. Nagging is so noisy, after all. And it never works. Permit God to develop that gentle, quiet spirit within you and eventually you may win your husband over without saying a word. You must be patient, though, and committed to changing your own viewing habits as an example. "Do as I say, not as I do" will get you nowhere—with your children or your husband.

Television certainly isn't the only source of nausea/noise in our homes. Many people listen to tapes, CDs, radio, etc., while driving or working around the house or yard, and there is nothing wrong with that. As I mentioned in chapter 9, listening to something we enjoy can brighten our spirits and make an unsavory task easier to tackle. The problem lies in thinking we *have* to have background sound. Some people say that they are uncomfortable when in perfect quiet and that they need to have the stereo, radio or TV on while they work.

May I be so bold as to suggest that this is nothing akin to a need? It is a habit, and though it would appear to be an innocuous one, I believe otherwise. There are at least three pitfalls to always having background entertainment within earshot. Perhaps you can think of more.

First, you need time alone with your thoughts. I can understand why an unbeliever would not wish to have such quiet time on her hands. Who wants to always be thinking about her sin and wondering about her eternal destiny? That is why the world is so incessantly loud. It is trying to drown out the conscience-stinging voice of a holy God. Even in situations where extraneous music or voices would be inappropriate, the world has on its headphones. If God is calling, it is certain He won't be heard. But the Christian has no such fearsome uncertainties, so why not live and work, at least some of the time, in quietness? Give God the opportunity to speak loving whispers to your heart. Aren't you interested in what His sweet Spirit is saying to you? Shouldn't you be thinking through some plans, formulating some goals? When are you going to do this—when you're sleeping? You may be one of the great thinkers of our age and no one, including you, will ever discover your profound mental ability because you can't even hear yourself think!

Another pitfall to the background noise bombardment is the fact that in order to survive in all of that racket, you and your family learn to tune things out. This is not a skill you wish to promote in your husband and children. Before long you will not be tuning out things; you will be tuning out *each other*. You do not want to be tuned out by your husband and children, do you?

You would never want to tune them out either. So you won't be offended if I remind you that you cannot listen to the talk show host and your eight-year-old at the same time. The host may be saying something of great interest to you, but it is your child who needs and deserves your undivided attention. Likewise, your teenager cannot possibly take in his CD and your verbal instructions.

So it's up to you. Turn off the TV. Turn off the CD. Get rid of the electronic babble and listen to what your loved ones are saying. You're the only wife and mother they have. Lend them your ear.

Besides being a distraction that prevents you from thinking, listening to God or hearing your loved ones, the constant drone of TV, videos and radio causes the development of another unfortunate habit—that of always raising your voice to be heard. No wonder some families are involved in a perpetual shouting match. Speaking loudly is a habit that is easy to form but difficult to break.

Before continuing, I want to make sure you understand my intentions here. I am not trying to convince you that you must tiptoe and whisper about your house as if it were a mortuary. Not at all! Your home should sometimes be filled with raucous laughter, squeals of delight and spirited music and conversation. But there also should be opportunities to enjoy peace and quiet, and many families today seem to have given up on that idea. I long for you to understand that it is unnecessary and undesirable to make that concession. If you would like to create a peaceful haven of your home, you most likely will need to make some changes, and who better than you to initiate those changes?

If you know that loud talking is a problem in your home, ask God to begin changing *you* first. Singers practice intoning. Cheerleaders practice leading cheers. Public speakers practice their inflections. You must practice speaking softly. Practice, practice, practice. Softly, incidentally, does not mean weakly, in a higher pitch or unclearly. You are not to change your voice; simply lower it. Just as you have over time (perhaps a lifetime) developed the habit of speaking too loudly, you can over time learn to speak softly. Ask God to help you. He is making you, at this very moment, into His own image. That surely entails speaking in a still, small voice.

Did you ever wonder why God chose that kind of voice with which to speak to His children? Could it be that a quiet voice communicates more effectively? We know in our hearts it is true, yet we speak to our own dear children in an angry, loud voice verging on, if not actually, screaming. What does this accomplish? Screaming begets more screaming, not the hoped-for compliance.

"The quiet words of the wise are more to be heeded than the shouts of a ruler of fools" (Eccl. 9:17). That is what God says. He knows that we wives and mothers will not be heard because of our shouting. We will not be obeyed because of our screaming. So He models for us a perfect parent's quietness. He guides, He instructs, He helps. And He always remembers our frame, that we are but dust, so when we fail and fall back into our old ways, He hasn't forgotten our efforts. He never scolds, screams or chides. He simply gives us a new beginning. Doesn't your heart leap with desire to please a parent like Him?

If you have been a screamer (most of us have if we will be honest), it is important to confess that sin to God and ask for His overcoming power to help. It is also important to confess it to your children, asking them to forgive you and explaining that you recognize the need to change that behavior. They will not view this as a sign of weakness on your part. Rather, they will identify with your struggle (they struggle too) and graciously forgive and revere you. Remember, it is never too early or too late to do right. Those who do not see a need for change in their lives do not see at all.

Remarkable things will begin to take place in your home as you permit God to have His way in this area of your life. As we discussed earlier, children mirror what they see—and hear. By precept and example you can teach your children the courtesy of speaking quietly. No one enjoys being around loud, obnoxious (notice how comfortably those adjectives fit together) people. Where will your children learn not to be loud and obnoxious but at home? You do them a terrible disservice if you neglect to train your little ones toward quietness.

That leads me to a final observation on the subject of quietness in the home. We all know that children are by nature loud, rowdy, uncivilized creatures. All of them come into the world in a self-centered rage and, adorable as they are, will never change on their own except to become more self-centered and more outraged.

Enter parents.

Unfortunately, many parents today fail to recognize what parents a generation or two ago took for granted: that parents exist for far more than the provision of love, food, shelter and clothing, as important as those things are. God has imbued parenthood with authority and given us the formidable task of civilizing the tiny creatures for this world and aiding them in becoming citizens of heaven.

That is why it shocks my sensibilities to hear parents say, "My child simply can't be still," or, "He can't be quiet for five minutes," or, "I could never take her into the church service with us. She can't stop talking." Of course the child can be still and quiet. It is against his nature but he can do it just the same. Only he won't, because it isn't *expected* of him. He hasn't been taught. He is not yet, at the age of 3 or 8 or (horrors) 12, civilized. Do you imagine that he will then become civilized, all by himself, at the age of 15 or 16?

Not only can young children be taught to speak quietly, but they can be trained to observe and enjoy quietness as well. Children do not need every hour of the day structured for them. They need time to listen, to observe nature, to be alone with their thoughts, to be alone with God.

When I look back on my childhood I recognize that the best gift God gave to me was solitude. Sounds boring, doesn't it? But as I sat beneath the branches of the willow tree in my tiny backyard on a towel or a scrap of a blanket or on the warm, moist earth, my thoughts frequently turned to God. I wondered about Him, about how I could get to know Him, where He might be found. I thought about the things I had done wrong, and how I wished I could stop doing those things. I observed the beauty of sunlight filtered through lacy willow leaves, and watched clumsy, orange elm bark beetles teeter like high-wire artists across slender blades of grass.

Those lonely childhood days were a far more valuable gift than being shuttled from lessons to games to play groups would have been, though I didn't know it then.

Your children have no idea what is best for them, either. You have to cut across their loud little natures, expect them to be capable of reasonable periods of quietness (we're not talking about eight-hour stretches of silence here), and then provide the opportunity for them to prove themselves capable.

Each family will have to decide for itself how and when to bring this about. I'll tell you how I did it simply as one example of the way it may be done. You know what will work best for your child.

As my children outgrew their need for afternoon naps, we continued having a "quiet hour" during that same period of time, usually right after lunch. Often I read to them at the start of the hour or we talked about something of interest to them. Then they were left to be quiet until a timer went off, which signaled that they could resume their usual work or play. They were not to come to me and ask if the time was up. Neither could they talk to each other or play together, though they could play quietly alone. They were not permitted to listen to radios or tapes. As they got older they often read to themselves or even fell asleep if they were tired. Sometimes they colored or wrote letters. Believe it or not, they began to look forward to their quiet hour each day. It was never viewed as punishment. It's not that they always would have chosen to be still and quiet for an hour, but it wasn't their choice. Authority simplifies so many things.

Your children need to appreciate silence as well as laughter, stillness as well as rollicking celebration. They need quiet time for meditation and rumination. They need solitude so that they might learn to appreciate the company of God. They need the discipline of self-restraint and resisting their natural inclinations.

And the world needs children—*and adults*—for whom these needs have been wisely supplied.

F. W. Robertson stated the importance of quietness this way: "Meditation is done in silence. By it we renounce our narrow individuality, and expatiate into that which is infinite. Only in the sacredness of inward silence does the soul truly meet the secret hiding God. The strength of resolve which afterwards shapes life, and mixes itself with action, is the fruit of those sacred, solitary moments. There is a divine depth in silence. We meet God alone."[1]

Now I'm going to quit yammering about quietness and actually give you some. Peace be unto you and yours, my Child.

O Thou Who art my quietness, my deep repose,
My rest from strife of tongues, my holy hill,
Fair is Thy pavilion, where I hold me still.
Back let them fall from me, my clamorous foes,
Confusions multiplied;
From crowding of sense I flee, and in Thee hide.
Until this tyranny be overpast,
Thy hand will hold me fast;
What though the tumult of the storm increase,
Grant to Thy servant strength, O Lord, and bless with peace.
— Amy Carmichael

Very slight things make epochs in married life.

—George Eliot

11

"He Can Stir His Own Coffee"

The test of the life of a saint is not success, but faithfulness in human life as it actually is. We will set up success in Christian work as the aim; the aim is to manifest the glory of God in human life, to live the life hid with Christ in God in human conditions. Our human relationships are the actual conditions in which the ideal life of God is to be exhibited.—Oswald Chambers[1]

I sat in the tiny waiting room of the dentist's office, answering the stack of correspondence I had brought along, as my younger two children were having their six-month checkup and cleaning. All of my mental faculties were engaged in completing my letter-writing task until the name of an old, long-lost friend crashed my concentration. It startled me back into consciousness of the goings-on around me, and I realized I had heard the office manager speak the name to someone on the telephone. I listened intently to her end of the conversation and soon understood that she was speaking to a health insurance representative. My dear friend Emily must have recently been in for treatment! Could it be that she was back and living in the area after all these years? My heart raced with excitement as I considered how joyous a reunion with Brad and Emily Scott (not their real names) and their children would be after such a long separation. I was flooded with happy memories of our comradeship with that family.

Those were years of happy busyness for all of us. The Scotts had three young children and, for a while, a foster child. We had two at first, with numbers three and four arriving later. We attended the same church and were drawn to each other in that curious way of friendship that remembers no beginning and knows no end. We loved Brad and Emily and they us. It was an easy kind of friendship, the make-no-pretense, drop-in-anytime kind that resembles family love more than some family relationships do.

Brad and David were both handymen extraordinaire. Brad had more experience than David in woodworking, and I remember him giving up some Saturdays to help David with a making-room-for-baby addition on the brick ranch we owned then. Both men were family-oriented, godly, quiet gentlemen who got along famously. It was a delight to see them working side by side on various projects. Brad was a big help to David. We always felt indebted to him.

If David and Brad were well suited for friendship, Emily and I were more so. We were both wives and mothers above all else, loved our families with fiery intensity, and most of our conversations were happily centered around our husbands and little ones. We did share some other interests, though, including art and music. Emily was an accomplished artist and she gave me many helpful tips for my art dabbling. She taught me the basics for mixing paint colors, for example, and she had wonderful ideas for using original artwork in the home. Emily also possessed a sweet, clear soprano voice, which she always used to glorify her Savior. I never saw anyone look as reverent as Emily did when she sang. I wanted to be like her. It's uplifting to have a friend worthy of emulation.

Our fellowship with that couple was a bright spot in those years of diapers, spilled milk, skinned knees and runny noses. Brad and Emily gave us a great deal. I honestly don't remember giving them much in return, except perhaps a bit of adult conversation in the midst of a torrent of toddler talk. But they cherished us just the same.

There was one indisputable problem, though. It hardly seems worth mentioning after such fond remembrances, but one thing made us more than a little uncomfortable while in the Scotts' company. As giving, loving, understanding and accepting as they were with us and nearly everyone else, they were incredibly trite and nitpicking with each other. Isn't that amazing? And it is all the more amazing in view of the fact that it was apparent to all who knew them that they adored each other. When Emily sang in church, Brad appeared enraptured. Emily always demonstrated pride in Brad's handiwork. They enjoyed one another's humor and shared many interests. But once in their presence for any length of time, it was obvious that both had the immature habit of challenging nearly everything the other said. I'm not speaking of important information that if repeated incorrectly would inconvenience or mislead someone. Rather, they would challenge the most insignificant details of each other's speech. Brad might say, "We had to wait in line for thirty minutes at the bank last night." Emily's immediate retort would be, "It wasn't thirty minutes, Brad. It was twenty-three minutes."

The two would go on endlessly that way, all the while being perfectly cordial to us. Tension mounted between them until *our* stomachs were in knots. Eventually they would leave and we always wondered how much the argument would escalate before they called it quits. The next time we saw them they would be fine—cheerful and pleasant with us and each other— for a while. Then, if Emily said something like, "Do you remember how gorgeous it was last Wednesday? We took the kids to the beach," Brad would inevitably respond, "That wasn't Wednesday, it was Tuesday."

My reminiscing ended abruptly when the office manager finished her telephone conversation and hung up. I set aside my stationery and pen and walked over to her desk.

"I couldn't help overhearing parts of your conversation," I confessed. "I think you mentioned the name of an old friend of mine, Emily Scott. We lost track of Brad and Emily years ago. Are they back in the area?"

"Yes," she replied. "At least Emily and the kids are back. I don't think Brad is with them anymore."

My joy at rediscovering a precious friend shattered at the news of her failed marriage. In spite of all their petty bickering, I was shocked to learn that Brad and Emily had parted ways. I always had hoped that those two dear people would eventually outgrow their argumentative tendencies for the sake of their marriage and their children. Plainly, that wasn't the case.

Since that day at the dentist's office I've thought often about Brad and Emily. I've prayed for them both and wondered where Brad is now and how it must be for him, the man we knew as a devoted husband and father, possibly hundreds of miles away from his wife and nearly grown children. My heart aches as I think about something as wonderful and full of possibilities as their marriage going so dreadfully wrong.

I've also remembered other incidents, behaviors and symptoms of trouble that escaped me so many years ago when I was inexperienced and less mature myself. Now, in retrospect, I can see how damaging to their relationship these behaviors were.

Already you have seen that Brad and Emily were each unwilling to give an inch. No subject or detail was too trivial for a dispute. This weakness carried over into what they did for each other as well, yet nothing would have been too much for us to ask of them. In friendship, they were sacrificial, but to relinquish individual rights or sacrifice for the sake of each other didn't often happen.

Since I talked far more with Emily than with Brad, I recognized these traits more in her, though Brad demonstrated them at times too. One conversation I had with Emily burns brightly in my memory. I wish I had known to say to her then the things I am trying to impress on you now. But I was just learning it myself, so I was no help at all to my beloved friend.

At the time I was expecting our third child while running after a preschooler and a toddler. David and I were staying up late most nights working on our room addition, and we always arose before dawn in order for David to reach his job on time.

The best I can remember, I was pretty tired most of the time and, occasionally, exhausted. This troubled Emily and she was wise to advise me to take better care of myself. Some of her advice was most unwise, however, and revealed her unwillingness to make personal sacrifices in her relationship to her husband.

"Why do you get up with David in the morning? You don't need to get up so early; you *need* more sleep." I can still picture her cheerful kitchen, decorated with a strawberry motif, where we sat and sipped tea as our children played in the next room.

I told her that I liked being with David in the morning and that I also felt he shouldn't have to face a hard day's work without a good breakfast. What she said to me then has never left me. These were her exact words: "Well, I sure don't get up with Brad in the morning. I need my sleep. He's not a baby. He can pour milk on his own corn flakes and he can stir his own coffee."

My face flushed as it dawned on me that Emily was hyperbolizing to make her point, when I actually did prepare David's cup of coffee just the way he liked it and stirred it for him before he came into the kitchen. I felt silly and wondered if I was babying my husband as Emily implied. But it didn't cause me to change the way I was doing things. I couldn't have explained why, but I was sure Emily's attitude toward the little sacrifices of being a marriage partner was wrong. Now, after learning of her dissolved marriage, I'm thankful that God gave me that bit of discernment as a young wife.

You mustn't think for a moment that I was born with a single sacrificial bone in my body, or that I never struggled with selfishness in my marriage. On the contrary, I can be self-centered with the best of them and was immature when David and I married. There had been no fitting role model in my childhood home, and the attitudes formed in me were less than Christian, to say the least. Of course, my sin nature was thrown in the bargain too. I was a newborn Christian when we got married, and many of my sinful attitudes had not yet been transformed. I wanted my own way in just about everything, and I resented the dozens of sacrifices that were required of Mrs. David Revell but had never been required of Glenda. I even remember (to my shame) sitting on the living room floor one day crying because I was having a hard time matching David's socks. The black and navy and dark green ones looked just alike to me, and he was always telling me—not in a complaining way, but it felt to me as if he were complaining—that his socks didn't match. I recall thinking, *Why in the world do I have to match these stupid socks? I hate it. I don't want to do it.*

Can you believe that? Consider the whole picture: David faithfully got up and went to work every morning, facing an increasingly stressful job in order to provide enough so that I might be able to stay at home as we both desired, and I resented having to match his clean socks! I freely admit it to you that I was a wretch.

So what was it that changed me, transformed my thinking, revolutionized my love? You know already, don't you? It was Jesus Christ. He alone has the power to make us what we were meant to be. His work is always within the context of our yieldedness, though. As I said before, He is powerful, but He is a gentleman. He knocks and waits, knocks and waits, knocks and waits. Always He is interceding for us, planning our obedience and equipping us for success. And He knocks and waits.

Do you hear Him? You can ignore the knocking. It's always your choice. I did that for a while, but I need to warn you that was a miserable choice.

Anyone who knows us now would find it hard to believe, but David and I had a tremendously difficult start to our marriage. It is nothing less than a miracle that it survived the first two years. I'd rather not tell this, but for the sake of both helping you and truthfulness, I must. Most of the problems we had were my fault.

David and I were madly in love when we got married, at least we thought we were. Looking back I would have to say that David truly did love me. He was mature, and his love enabled him to make many sacrifices on my behalf. I'll never cease thanking God for David's Christ-likeness in those early years. It saved our marriage.

I was sure I loved David as well, but I understand now that I was too immature and full of self to love anybody. I loved being loved. I loved the idea of being wanted by somebody. I loved myself. David fit into that picture of self-love quite nicely, so I thought I loved *him*. It was nearly two years after our wedding when I finally faced that ugly truth about myself. It was obvious much sooner than that, but we don't see what we don't want to see, nor do we hear what we don't want to hear. We squeeze our eyes shut to painful truth. We ignore the knocking.

If you have read my first book, *Glenda's Story: Led by Grace*, you know that I was sexually molested for about eight years in my childhood. While that was a horrible tragedy, God reached down in tenderness and love, saved my soul—*and* my life—and led me into a marriage that everyone agreed was "made in heaven." I had no idea before our wedding of the harmful sequelae from that abuse that I was bringing into our marriage. David had no idea either, because I had never told him about the abuse. I was far too ashamed of my past to want him to know anything of it. My "dirty little secret" would remain just that, I thought. *It won't affect me*, I assured myself. *God will take care of everything.*

Well, I was certainly right about *that*. But God had a far different way of taking care of the problem than I had imagined. He took care of it by using it to yield me to Himself. And because of my stubborn will, it took two long, painful years for Him to accomplish what He could have done in a moment. How revealing hindsight is!

As early as our honeymoon I realized I was in serious trouble. I couldn't, no matter how hard I tried, respond to David sexually. My pain, both physical and emotional, was paralyzing. It felt as if I had been dropped into the blackness of an abysmal pit with no hope of escape. My despair was unfathomable.

Imagine David's confusion and despair, not knowing what was wrong. He was kind. He was gentle. He was as understanding as a person with no information could be. His hurt and perplexity were second only to mine.

Do you know from where most anger arises? It springs forth from hurt. You see, pain makes us feel vulnerable. People who are hurting (which includes everyone at one time or another) already feel weak and want to escape not only the pain, but also the overwhelming feeling of vulnerability. So without conscious thought, the "weakness" of pain is converted to the "strength" of anger. We respond with anger because it feels safer than revealing the vulnerability of our pain. This is tragic, first, because it keeps us from facing and dealing with the actual cause of our problem and, second, because the person on the receiving end of our anger is frequently not the one who hurt us. Hence, I sat on the floor crying with anger over the injustice of having to fold David's socks when neither David nor his socks were the actual source of my pain.

Matters became far worse before they improved. My unfounded anger toward David grew and grew. I was aware that he hadn't caused the problem. But he was the one forcing me to acknowledge, if only to myself, that the problem existed. There I was with all of that inner turmoil, fearing the ultimate rejection—divorce—with no one to whom I could go for help and only one option in the whole world: strength through anger.

Had our story appeared under the familiar heading "Can This Marriage Be Saved?" the resounding and logical answer would have been no!

But one day an incredibly illogical thing happened. I came undone, to the end of my rope, to the end of myself. All of that misery had been a thickly veiled gift from God to bring me to the moment for which He had been so patiently waiting. At last, I heard Him knocking.

Vividly, I remember falling to my knees by our bed and pouring out to my knowing Father all the rancor, the striving, the anger, the *self*. Nothing was held back. It was unconditional surrender.

"Oh, God," I cried, "I cannot go on this way. I'm so sick of myself, of running from my past, of wanting my own way.

You've saved me from hell; now please save me from myself. I can't love David the way I am. Change me. Make me all over again. Fill me with love for him. Do anything to me that pleases You. I don't care how much it hurts. Nothing could be worse than living with my wretched self. In Jesus' name, Amen."

Do you imagine that I had to plead with my Father for an answer to that earnest prayer? I did not. He began the process of changing me that day. He's still at work now, 20 years later, and I couldn't be more thankful. But the most miraculous (no other word will suffice) aspect of His work was the deep, vast, profound love that He poured forth through me to David *that very day* and every day since. My angry, hurting heart of stone became God's soft, fleshly vessel of love—not the gushy, sentimental, motion-picture sort of love either.

This love of which I speak is slow to lose patience—it looks for a way of being constructive. It is not possessive; it is neither anxious to impress nor does it cherish inflated ideas of its own importance. . . . Love has good manners and does not pursue selfish advantage. It is not touchy. It does not keep account of evil or gloat over the wickedness of other people. On the contrary, it shares the joy of those who live by the truth. . . . Love knows no limits to its endurance, no end to its trust, no fading of its hope, it can outlast anything. Love never fails. (1 Cor. 13:4-8, Phillips)

As a result, nothing has been the same in our home since that day. Whether matching David's socks, folding his clothes, cleaning our home, preparing his meals, stirring his coffee or, the utmost sacrifice for me, giving myself to him as we became one flesh, my joy has reached ultimate fullness. That is because of the paradox of which my own spiritual mother spoke when she said, "The measure of self-giving is the measure of fulfillment."[2] Selfishness *never* results in even temporary joy. Only in selflessness are we satisfied.

I hope you have understood that all the changes God wrought, He wrought in *me*. He didn't change David. He didn't change my circumstances either. The marriage bed was still uncomfortable for me. God *could* have completely removed that hindrance had He willed it. "The secret is Christ in me, not me in a different set of circumstances."[3]

He taught me that love doesn't avoid, but hears and endures all things and turns those once-hated "all things" into fodder for sacrifice. That, my Friend, is the resurrection life of Jesus . Christ, and it is mysteriously nothing but joy. In his devotional book *My Utmost for His Highest*, Oswald Chambers wrote, "Any problem, and there are many, that is alongside me while I obey God, increases my ecstatic delight, because I know that my Father knows, and I am going to watch, and see how He unravels this thing."[4]

Those were the lessons God had begun teaching me back in the days when Emily and I shared a rich friendship. I didn't understand all that had transpired in my life and had no idea how to express that which I *did* understand. Had that not been the case, I might have been able to help Emily recognize her own anger and her resentment concerning all it meant to be Brad's wife. Perhaps she could have seen her fiercely independent spirit the way God sees it. "We deify independence and willfulness and call them by the wrong name. What God looks on as obstinate weakness, we call strength."[5]

We all have those same tendencies, don't we? Have you seen yourself in any of this? Are you longing for change?

"I want change all right," you might say to me. "I want my husband changed. And if you knew him you'd understand why."

Will you listen intently to me now, my Daughter? Pay very close attention to what I'm about to say. The success of your marriage depends on your understanding this vital fact: *Neither you nor I can change your husband.* You can spend the rest of your life trying, but your years will be wasted; you will end up a frustrated, miserable wreck.

I'm not denying that your husband may sorely need changing, and if he is hurting you and I thought it would do a shred of good, I'd give him "what for" such as you cannot imagine! But it would do nothing but harm, so I am left to address only you.

God *can* change your husband and it is perfectly acceptable for you to pray along those lines. How and when God chooses to answer your prayers, however, is none of your business. It is *His* business, and He doesn't need any assistance whatsoever.

So what do you do in the meantime? You permit the Father to change *you*. You needn't wait until you are in bitter anguish of soul as I did. He's always waiting, always ready to answer that prayer. And after the transforming work begins, you may notice that, in spite of your husband's cantankerousness, the general mood of your entire household is improved. That is because of the indisputable fact that women set the tenor of the home. "If mama ain't happy, ain't nobody happy!" the quaint, true saying goes. Let God first work out His good and perfect will in you and see how you may win your husband without a word.

"Many make the household, but only one the home," said James Russell Lowell. And guess what? You're the one. And your attitude toward your husband is the whole crux of the matter. What do you want—vexation or peace? Bitterness or joy? A house or a home? Why don't you submit to an attitude alteration right now? Why not become a channel for the love of God in your marriage? What will you have if you don't?

When I surrendered my will to God's, all of my thinking was turned upside-down. I didn't worry anymore about my rights, or that I might be taken advantage of, or that I could end up giving more in our relationship than I received. None of those things was even a consideration. The love of God is boundless; it is no less boundless when poured through our bound-up hearts. The change it wrought in my behavior toward David was dizzying. How I loved him then! Bring on all the black, navy and green socks in the world! Nothing could be enough for me to do for my beloved David. The love of God transforms chores into privileges.

It may help you to know some of the practical lessons that transforming love has taught me over the years. Not that I want you to be following any list of "must dos"—mine or anyone else's. There is no power in that. Your strength is in the life hidden with

Christ. Changes must come from within and are brought about through submission of your will to God's.

Perhaps, though, you will be encouraged by someone else's pilgrimage, so I will tell you a few of the changes God made in me. Use them as a springboard for your own imagination. Only you know the things that would please your husband.

Incidentally, don't imagine for a moment that your husband will fall at your feet in gratitude for all the little (or big) things you do. He won't. He may not even seem to notice. That is of no concern to you. Remember, "love does not pursue selfish advantage."

God impressed upon me right away that I needed to be a better listener to my husband. David is a man of few words. The few he speaks are important clues in my lifelong enterprise of really getting to know and understand him. He needs for me to hear him rather than think about how I'm going to reply. Sometimes he just needs a sounding board. If I do not meet that legitimate need, then who will?

The unwise habits of Brad and Emily and other couples we knew helped me to consider the fact that no one likes to be corrected in the presence of others. If correction of a statement is absolutely necessary—say, if David is giving directions to someone and I think he is in error—I try to do it privately. If the error is a non-essential detail, then I try very hard to say nothing. There is no purpose whatsoever in arguing over or amending trivia. It is the unprofitable sport of the immature.

It is also imperative to never say the smug, "I told you so." If it takes biting off your tongue to avoid it, so be it. It's that important.

While God was teaching me that lesson of knowing when to keep my mouth shut, He was concurrently instructing me in the science of knowing when to speak up. The less I restricted the flow of God's love through me, the more I began to see David through God's eyes. This revealed to me many of David's wonderful attributes to which I had been blind before. The Holy Spirit nudged me then to point them out to others, both in David's presence and apart from it. This, I have discovered, serves many purposes.

First, it brings glory to God, who created my husband and gave him to me. Next, it is a breath of fresh air in a world where one-liners and put-downs have become the usual discourse, even among Christians.

Also, David receives affirmation when he hears me testify before others of how much he means to me, how much I admire his abilities and how much I appreciate his willingness to use those abilities to enhance our family life. I try to say these things privately too. But sincere public praise does wonders for a relationship and tends to elicit a like response. Over time, it can produce phenomenal change in attitudes.

If you and your husband have had more than your share of differences lately, you may have to look hard to find something in him to compliment. Go ahead and make the effort. There has to be *something* good you can say about him. He was good enough for you to enter into an "until death do us part" covenant with him, wasn't he? Ask God to remind you of the characteristics that drew you to your husband in the first place. Pray for the ability to see him with the compassionate vision of Christ. Then swallow your pride and praise the man as God has shown you. And don't be surprised by the revolution that may result, but do enjoy it.

I want to add here that we, as Christians, always should say what we believe. Whether or not that is true of us, one thing is sure—we will *believe* what we say. The more we find fault, criticize and harangue, the more we see with which to find fault, criticize and harangue. Don't do it. You'll only destroy your marriage and wind up submerged in the acid of bitterness. Have the courage to submit yourself to the sweetening Spirit of Christ. "Let this mind be in you which was also in Christ Jesus," the Bible tells us (Phil. 2:5, KJV). May I add my voice to the apostle Paul's as he wrote:

> Now if you have known anything of Christ's encouragement and of his reassuring love; if you have known some-

thing of the fellowship of his Spirit, and of compassion and deep sympathy, do make my joy complete—live together in harmony, live together in love, as though you had only one mind and one spirit between you. Never act from motives of rivalry or personal vanity, but in humility think more of each other than you do of yourselves. None of you should think only of his own affairs, but consider other people's interests also. (Phil. 2:1-4, Phillips)

You won't find better marriage counseling anywhere.

You've seen what God taught me about speaking up and shutting up. Now I'll tell you what He showed me to do.

The more I fell in love with my husband, the more my desire was toward pleasing him. I began to truly look forward to his return home each night. I wanted him to look forward to it, too, so I formed habits that I thought would produce that effect. For one thing, I always straightened the house in the late afternoon, and later, even when the children were quite small, toys were picked up and neatly stored before their daddy's arrival. He never asked us to do this, and I'm not sure he ever realized we did. But it impressed upon the children that their daddy was a very special man and that his homecoming each day was an *event*, and he had the benefit, whether he knew it or not, of finding neatness and order rather than chaos after a hard day's work.

I also tried to have myself looking at least presentable when David came home by brushing my hair, putting on fresh make-up and, if necessary, fresh clothes.

The children, too, met him with clean hands and faces and neatly brushed hair. When they were very little we had only one car, and David rode the bus to work. On pleasant days I walked the children to the bus stop to wait for "the big blue bus" that brought their daddy home. They would be bursting with excitement by the time he stepped off the bus. In return, he showed more than a little pride at having everyone on the bus see his doting family each day. I know it made a difference in his hard workday.

You may be thinking, *This is all right for you with your good husband, but my husband is a jerk. Do you really think I should try to make our children believe he is anything else?*

I am immensely sorry that you do not have a husband like mine. How I wish I could put my arms around you and comfort you and make everything better! But you cannot fool your children about their daddy. Children are far too smart for that. Apparently *you* were fooled by him, because you did choose to marry him. They have him as their father by no choice of their own, and now you must make the best of the situation for yourself and for them. Remember, children are commanded to honor their mothers and their fathers. That commandment is not negated when parents are inconsiderate or unkind. Therefore, you must do everything possible to help your children to revere their father. You can best do this by revering him yourself. I can only suggest this to you. God has commanded it: "The wife must respect her husband" (Eph. 5:33). He will empower you to respect your husband, if you are willing, and show you how.

Back to my husband's arrival home from work. His job provides for me the greatest gift he could possibly give: the privilege of staying at home with our children. Shouldn't I at least be there for him when he comes home? He has never demanded it, but I have always made it a priority. Of course there are times when it is impossible, when traffic or a doctor's appointment or some other engagement detains me. But as a general rule, I am there with some semblance of supper in the making when he drives up. He can count on it.

Others count on it, too, as I learned one day to my amazement when out-of-town friends dropped by while I was grocery shopping. They saw a neighbor out in her yard and asked if she knew how long I was going to be out. "No," she replied, "I don't know where she went today. But I'm sure she'll be home by 4:30. That's when David gets home from work and she's always home before him."

Interesting, isn't it, the things people notice about us? Our attitudes and behaviors, good or bad, exert more influence than we care to imagine. "Be very careful, then, how you live—not as unwise but as wise, making the most of every opportunity, because the days are evil. Therefore do not be foolish, but understand what the Lord's will is" (Eph. 5:15-17).

Something that I still struggle with but try to do for David is to hold my tongue about non-emergency household or family problems until after we've eaten supper. This is one kindness he *has* requested because his mind is still digesting work-related troubles and he needs a chance to discharge some of that stress before taking on more. This is the hardest thing in the world for me because I'm a talker in the first place, and I've been saving up all my stresses and problems all day long to talk about with him. But in this two-decade trial I have improved, I think. Waiting to talk is a small sacrifice, anyway, when love rules.

Besides trying to anticipate and meet my husband's expectations, I've learned the very important, stress-relieving tactic of lowering mine. Most of the difficulties that occur early in marriage are caused by unrealistic expectations. As a result of reading too many fairy tales as a child, a woman believes that all of her emotional needs will be met by her handsome prince every day of the year. As a result of never growing up and leaving the self-centeredness of boyhood, a man thinks that she loves hearing about his mother's wonderful cooking and longs, with all of her heart, to someday match those heretofore unrivaled culinary skills. It won't be long before both are disappointed, disillusioned and disgusted. And no wonder. Life is no fairy tale. Marriage is no picnic.

It may not sound very romantic, but it's easier to build a successful relationship when we don't expect an awful lot of each other, especially at first. Then there's less room for disappointment. The flip side of this arrangement is also helpful. When you stop expecting your husband to be perfect, you realize that *you* don't have to be perfect either. What a relief! Even the best marriage is nothing more than a partnership between two very imperfect people—*sinners*, actually.

I still remember my shock at discovering that marriage is not a never-ending pajama party. Before our wedding I had imagined that we would lie in bed long into the night discussing our goals and our dreams. David had imagined that we would lie in bed at night and sleep. He won.

The greatest favor we can ever bestow on our spouses is to turn our expectations of them on ourselves. In other words, instead of longing for an ideal mate, *become one*. And since every couple is unique, only you know what that "becoming" will require of you. That is what makes marriage the hard work and exciting adventure that it is.

Major attitude adjustments aside, it's a multitude of little things that make all the difference in relationships: the tone of voice we consistently use, our body language, simple courtesies, patience, willingness to forgive. "Remember, very slight things make epochs in married life," George Eliot said.[6]

Whether it be very slight things God is asking of you, very great things or both, please listen to His voice. The world's vain, deceptive message to you as a wife will be a far cry from His. He made you. He made your husband. He created marriage. He wants only the best for you, His dearly loved child, and this is what He says to you: "Whoever wants to save his life will lose it, but whoever loses his life for me will save it" (Luke 9:24).

Every day in your marriage you are given the chance to "lose" your life for Jesus Christ. Don't forfeit this marvelous opportunity because of the silly notion that you can only be truly happy when *you* are being loved, when *you* are being cuddled, when *you* are being catered to. The exact opposite is true! Real joy comes only from self-giving. If you find that too hard to believe, why don't you put it to the test? Think of some little sacrifice you could make on behalf of your soon-to-be-shocked-out-of-his-socks husband and do it. And while you're dreaming up that selfless surprise, why don't you go ahead, wake up and stir his coffee. Epochs are made from such a slight thing as this.

> Father of spirits, this my sovereign plea
> I bring again and yet again to Thee,

Fulfil me now with love that I may know
A daily inflow, daily overflow.

For love, for love my Lord was crucified,
With cords of love He bound me to His side.

Pour through me now: I yield myself to Thee,
Love, blessed Love, do as Thou wilt with me.

— Amy Carmichael

Precious memories are not about anything money can buy. They're about doing simple things with the people we love and the people who love us.

12

A Home Worth Remembering

If you wanted to gather up all tender memories, all lights and shadows of the heart, all banquetings and reunions, all filial, fraternal, paternal, conjugal affections, and had only just four letters with which to spell out the height and depth and length and breadth and magnitude and eternity of meaning, you would write it out with these four capital letters: HOME.—T. DeWitt Talmage

By now you most certainly have understood what some unfortunate people never learn: relationships, not furnishings, make a house a home. Of what value is a gilded mansion without the love of mother and father, son and daughter, brother and sister? Committing to do whatever God shows us to do in order to form and strengthen those relationships requires courage, honesty, work, fortitude, surrender and sacrifice, and not in small doses either. Building a home is a grueling labor of love, a never-ending assignment. Cowards and slackers need not apply.

I wouldn't have you think for a moment, though, that Christian home life is all drudgery. It is nothing of the sort! Anything worth having is worth working for, and healthy family relationships are certainly worth having. All of that intensity of effort pays rich dividends to those who endure the travail, and to their children after them; for it is out of those relationships that happy memories are birthed. Relationships are work; pleasant recollections of home are the natural result of that work. The memory-making itself is virtually effortless.

Some families get it all backwards. They ignore the deep trouble that exists in their relationships while investing a wealth of time and money orchestrating events for their families. The results are less than gratifying.

Though most children would be unable to articulate it, there is not a child on earth who wouldn't prefer just spending time at home with two parents who enjoy a loving relationship over going on a dozen costly excursions with angry, disagreeable folks. But earning the money to take a child to an expensive theme park is far easier than working through interpersonal perplexities, so many parents spring for the theme park and hope for the best.

You would never dream of doing such a foolish thing, I know. If that were your mind, you never would have made it so far in this book. My heart swells with pride when I think of all the work you've done and are continuing to do to please God in your relationships and in your home. Do not lose heart. God will never forget your work; your labor is not in vain.

While setting about trying to make beautiful memories for your children, you may realize more and more how few you have from your own childhood. Do not permit that realization to depress or preoccupy you. Not a thing can be done to change it. No one in your life now can make it up to you. Childhood is not repeatable. Parents don't get a second chance. Perhaps they did the best they could, or perhaps in some cases they really didn't care. Maybe they even *meant* it for evil. So what? God meant it for good. Accept the portion you have been given with submissive grace and permit Him to rechannel your hurt and disappointment into the energy required to do a better job for *your* children. Your lack of good memories need not stand in the way of your bestowing a joyous heritage on your offspring. Rather, it can become the impetus for it. You must remember that the family from which you came is not nearly so important as the family you now have or will have. Seize the opportunity at hand–there is no other.

If your memory is filled with warm and happy images from childhood, you already have a springboard from which you can launch your family's good times. I would remind you, though, that every family unit is unique and you can never re-create some other family's style in your home. Family amusements and rituals must be tailor-made for the family experiencing them. Forced fun flops.

One thing everyone, regardless of background, needs to remember is the perfect home or the perfect family does not exist. There will always be not-so-good days and perfectly wretched days. As long as these days are the exception, you needn't worry that all is lost. The raw truth is children misbehave, dogs bite, cars break down, goldfish die, parents lose it—and everyone survives. (Well, everyone except the goldfish.) These family foibles simply prepare us for life in the real world and teach us to adjust. Children know when they are loved, and "love covers over a multitude of sins" (1 Pet. 4:8). Children are a fairly resilient breed, as well. How else do you think any of us made it this far? Keep your sense of humor and learn to stop thinking of minor upsets and disappointments as crises and tragedies. Relax a little, roll with the punches, and throw your head back and laugh every now and then. Who knows? Maybe your child's warmest memory will be of the day everything that could go wrong did and his mama laughed until tears rolled down her cheeks. Then again, he may end up like humorist Dave Barry, who said, "Those boyhood memories! I have them often, although I can control them pretty well with medication!"

The thing I most want to emphasize to you, my Daughter, is the fact that pleasant memories cannot be purchased with any amount of money. Many young couples today miss the boat on this and often it is because they want *so badly* to give good memories to their children. If a mother has few treasurable memories from her childhood, she may be even more determined than the average mom to see to it that her children don't grow up the same way. This can lead to a frantic effort to create something that occurs quite naturally *without* the effort. So she spends large sums of money for extravagant vacations, parties and toys. "It costs more to amuse a child than it did to educate his father," someone said. Please listen to me. Parties, vacations and toys are not the stuff of which childhood memories are made. *Memories are created from time spent with those who are important to us.*

You're not sure you believe that, are you? Well, don't just take my word for it. Ask some people you know and admire what is their fondest childhood memory. I did that myself, inquiring of more than a dozen people of assorted ages and different walks of life. I did not tell any of them the premise I was out to prove until after they gave me their answers. The results delighted me.

Why not sit back and relax, have another cup of tea and vicariously enjoy some special childhood moments as you read the happy responses I received.

From my next-door neighbor and friend, Frances Delk, age 54: "I think my happiest memory is of our family picnics. Every summer family would come to our house from all over the area—even from as far away as Richmond—and everyone would bring loads of food. We would set up makeshift tables in the backyard out of boards laid across sawhorses, and we would all just have the best time together. We played games and some of my cousins would even dress up in old-fashioned clothes, bathing suits and hats. It was so much fun!"

From author, public speaker, former missionary to Ecuador and my own spiritual mother, Elisabeth Elliot Gren, 71: "That's one of those questions that's impossible to answer! I guess it would have to be our family visits each summer to Gale Cottage in Franconia, New Hampshire." (Gale Cottage was built by Elisabeth's Uncle Will and fully described in her book *All That Was Ever Ours* and again in *The Shaping of a Christian Family*, where she says, "It was to me as the very vestibule of heaven.")

"Another wonderful memory is of my father's walks with us children on weekend afternoons. That is when he gave us botany lessons and taught us bird calls." Elisabeth describes such walks in *The Shaping of a Christian Family* this way: "My father's recreation nearly always included his children. We could count on his doing something with us on Saturday afternoons—walks to the Walnut Lane Bridge or to Thomas's Place in Fairmont Park where he would miraculously 'find' Saltines in the hallow of a tree. A Saltine was a treat for us in those days, and very exciting when extracted from a tree or perhaps from an unsuspecting boy's pocket. . . . And so we children were shaped."

From Dr. Oran Chenault, 63, my longtime physician and friend: "I think it would have to be the Sunday afternoon drives our family always took. I have very fond memories of those."

From Phillip Hardison, 31, police captain and family friend: "One thing that really stands out in my memory was when I was eight or nine years old. I had a motorcycle, and my grandmother, who must have been in her late fifties then, against everybody's better judgment got on the back of that motorcycle with me and I drove her all over the farm. Also, we spent time every summer with our grandparents in their home in North Carolina. It was just us, together with them, at their home. That is a very special memory to me."

From my friend Donna Otto, 51, who is an author and public speaker: "I still remember how excited I was the day I went to my Aunt Pat's house for my first knitting and crocheting lessons. She had insisted that I wait until she thought I was old enough to learn. When I arrived, she had everything ready and waiting for me, including a huge ball of red yarn. I made from that yarn a bright red, indescribably ugly muffler, but that is a wonderful memory for me."

From Donald B. Woodby, 73, a dear friend and former pastor of mine: "I would say it is the memory of going fishing with my mom and dad and brothers and catching a huge catfish."

From Harriet Heath, 60, my dear friend and a retired public school teacher who taught music to me in high school: "I think my fondest memory—or at least one of my fondest—is

194 With Love From a Mother's Heart

that of going with my parents to Massanetta Springs (a rambling campground and conference center in the beautiful Blue Ridge Mountains of Virginia), where they attended a Bible conference every summer. I have wonderful memories of our times together there."

From Joni Eareckson Tada, 47, artist, author, public speaker and courageous victim of a spinal cord injury who was left paralyzed from the neck down and has spent 30 years in a wheelchair: "I have very early memories of my dad stirring up my interest in art. Often when he was busy at his easel mixing oils and painting on his canvas, I'd sit on the floor at his side with my crayons and coloring book and work just as hard as he was. He'd set his brushes aside, reach down and lift me up onto his lap. He would then fix my hand on one of his brushes and enfold his larger, stronger hand around mine. Then he'd guide my hand and the brush, dipping it into the palette and mixing burnt umber and raw siennas. We would stroke the wet, shiny paint on the canvas before us, and I'd watch with amazement.

"I also love the crazy, wonderful way my mother raised my sisters and me. I remember the time she turned off the oven, untied her apron and called us to walk with her to watch the sunset. The brilliant splash of pink and purple will stick in my mind forever."

From Brenda Kallaher, 53, registered nurse and my close friend: "I remember when I was very young, before starting school, riding the bus downtown with Mama every Friday. The purpose of the trip was to pay bills, I think, but we also visited other businesses—all the big department stores and little shops, and then, for the crowning treat of the whole trip, we would visit a lunch counter in the Professional Building and enjoy a meal together before catching the bus back home. Those were the only meals that we ever ate out during my entire growing-up years, so it was very special to me. I always thought it was great fun and it's one of my warmest memories."

From Dr. Donald E. Soles, 34 our family physician and friend: "I would have to say it was camping at the beach every summer with my parents and younger brother. We would go fishing, crabbing and scalloping. We always went to Emerald Isle, which is south of the Outer Banks of North Carolina. It was only thirty minutes from home, but we had to take the ferry to get there so it seemed to me like we were going to the uttermost part of the earth.

"My mother would scrimp and save for weeks in order to buy special groceries for the trip—things we especially liked, such as little individual boxes of cereal. When the time came each year for us to return home, my brother and I would cry and cry. Some years our father would let us go ahead and stay another week and he would make the long commute back and forth to work every day. I realize now what a sacrifice that was, especially considering how much he disliked the heat.

"We did a lot of things together as a family while I was growing up, but I'd have to say those summers of camping on Emerald Isle are my fondest childhood memory."

From Lowell Davey, longtime friend, president of the Bible Broadcasting Network and one of the most dedicated family men I've ever known: "My favorite memory is of working with my father on the farm where I grew up. That was the best thing going."

The youngest people of whom I asked the question were my own daughters, Charlotte, 19, and Sarah, 18.

From Charlotte, a freshman at Bryan College in Dayton, Tennessee: "I think my very favorite memory is of the bonfires we used to have in the backyard on Saturday nights in the summertime. We always roasted marshmallows and listened to the drama *Unshackled* on a portable radio. Sarah and I would run around and play games in the dark, and we got to stay up a little later than usual. I always loved that."

From Sarah, a senior in high school: "I remember that we would occasionally have popcorn as a special treat. Daddy would place the popcorn popper on the kitchen table, where it was eye level with Charlotte and me. He poured oil and the popcorn in the bottom, put the clear plastic lid on and plugged it in. Charlotte and I always had a contest to find out who would see the first kernel pop. We kneeled in our chairs with elbows propped on the table, our faces held still by our hands as we watched intently until one kernel exploded, and we would immediately yell, 'POPcorn!' Usually we said it together, but every once in a while, one or the other of us would get it out first. That person won. Come to think of it, we didn't actually win anything—just the knowledge that we won. It was so much fun."

Do you see the pattern in all these testimonies? Do you recognize the theme? Even I didn't expect it to be so utterly clear. Precious memories are not about anything money can buy. They're about doing simple things with the people we love and the people who love us.

Let's look at it another way. If we add together the ages of everyone I interviewed, the grand total is 639 years. Think about it. These individuals have collectively celebrated 639 birthdays, Christmases and other holidays, yet not one of them expressed his or her fondest memory as "the Christmas I received a 21-speed bike," or "the year I had a huge birthday party in a rented hall," or "the vacation when we stayed at a five-star hotel and ate caviar." Several of my respondents undoubtedly have warm memories of holidays, special gifts received and super vacations. The standout memories, though, were always the time spent with family doing remarkably unremarkable things.

If you haven't started your family yet, or if your children are very young, this information could drastically simplify your future as a parent. Children do not need, nor is it desirable for them to have, expensive or elaborate amusements. Keep it simple. Be imaginative. Think like a child.

When I asked my four children for some reminders of things we did when they were small, I was surprised at some of the things they remembered as very special. Here are a few of their responses: "Peanut butter and jelly sandwiches every Sunday night after church." "Playing barefoot in summer rain showers."

"Snuggling up to read together every night." "Friday night flings." (We started those when the children were very small, and they always entailed going to McDonald's to play at the playground. Usually we ate supper at home and purchased ice cream cones at McDonald's for dessert. Sometimes we couldn't even buy ice cream, but we went to play on the playground anyway. On especially big fling nights, when we had an extra two dollars to spend on riotous living, before going home we drove the car through an automated car wash. This was a huge thrill for our children. I'm not kidding.) "Teddy bear picnics." (Sometimes on rainy days I would spread a blanket on the floor and invite the children to escort their favorite doll or stuffed animal to an indoor picnic lunch.) "Taking long walks together." "Going to watch the fireworks at our 'special spot' every July 4th." "Going to the mountains every fall." "Playing with the box our new refrigerator came in."

Sarah remembers one very hot summer afternoon when she and Charlotte, who were around three and four years old, respectively, were at a loss for something to do. I put them in their bathing suits, drew water in the bathtub and let them play to their hearts' content with a 49¢ can of shaving cream. They squirted one another, made little foam snowmen and enjoyed a rousing, cool, clean time. The giggles and squeals from that afternoon are still fresh in our hearts.

The reason all of these very simple pleasures constituted memory-making thrills for our kids is because our circumstances had never permitted more. Not that we were poor, by any means. We always had everything we needed—and vastly more. But there wasn't extra money for extravagances, and now I look back on that as one of God's great mercies toward us. Had we been capable of lavishing our family with tangible treasures, I doubt we would have possessed the restraint necessary to avoid it. God restrained us, though, and I'm glad. Our children are far from perfect, but one characteristic that they each seem to be developing as they mature is a deep sense of sincere gratitude for even the tiniest loving gesture. And they are as undemanding as they are thankful. That makes a mother's heart glad.

Perhaps your children are beyond the toddler stage and you realize that your emphasis has been too much on the things money can buy. You'd like to change direction, but it almost seems impossible. Let me assure you, Daughter, it is *quite* possible. Not that you won't meet resistance on every side, mind you. It's much easier to teach children a little self-denial when one starts early. Still, it's never too late to do right. Prayer would be an excellent starting point for this blessed endeavor.

If you're really serious about weaning your family off of the costly amusement habit, you'll have to be ready with some fanciful substitutes. Perhaps some of the ideas already presented in this chapter will jump-start your imagination. God, whom we all know is unusually creative, will certainly guide and help you. He will "turn the hearts of the fathers to their children, and the hearts of the children to their fathers" (Mal. 4:6). It will be immensely less difficult for Him to accomplish this if the fathers and the children (and the mothers too) aren't glued to that vacuous, value-devoid television set. I've read stories about families who turn the tube off for a predetermined period of time— a week or a month or one day every week—and pass the time they would ordinarily spend in an electronic coma on some enjoyable family activity.

Less time in front of the TV also provides the added benefit of removing a major source of "the wants and the gimmies" from your home. You don't imagine, do you, that advertisers employ any scruples whatsoever in the battle for your children's hearts and your wallet? Convincing people that they must make certain purchases in order to be fulfilled is *what they do for a living!* The fact that children are particularly susceptible to this message has not gone unnoticed by them. But as powerful as that message may be, you are more powerful still—if, of course, you engage the services of the off button.

As you do more and more things together as a family, you'll begin to notice that some activities really seem to fit you. These are the things that your children will request over and over again, or that you and your husband will automatically repeat because you observed everyone's enjoyment of it. When this happens, not only are you making memories, you are establishing *traditions.*

Look back over the childhood memories of my friends and children. Notice how frequently they used the words *every* and *always.* In those cases the memory is of some custom or tradition rather than a one-time fun time. Traditions are powerful bonding agents and memory makers. Children love them and derive a sense of security and belonging from them. Listen as your children tell their friends, "We go there *every* summer," or, "We *always* do it this way." And if you still doubt that traditions really matter that much to your child, just try to change one and see what happens. If your children are anything like mine, you'll hear a loud refrain of, "But we *have* to do it that way. It's tradition!"

Traditions can be serious or silly, simple or complicated. We typically associate traditions with holidays and religious observances, and those traditions truly are splendid. Going to church together as a family, observing the Lord's Supper regularly, reading the Bible and praying together, discussing God's laws with your children "when you sit at home and when you walk along the road, when you lie down and when you get up" (Deut. 6:7)—all of these practices serve to impress upon the hearts of your children those truths and values that you hold most dear. "And when [they] are old [they] will not depart from it" (Prov. 22:6, KJV).

In addition to the marvelous traditions of our faith, everyday opportunities for the formation of family traditions are almost limitless. Anything can become a family tradition, from the way children are tucked in at night to the way butter beans are cooked. Most parents carry over a few traditions from their own childhood, and every family eventually generates traditions all their own.

Young parents can certainly plan ahead for some of the traditions they would like to observe as a family. "Let's always go to church on Christmas Eve," for example, or, "Let's take the kids to the beach for a week every summer." Often traditions spring out of something that was only intended to be a one-time occasion. Our family's favorite tradition began that way.

When our youngest son, Daniel, was a baby and Christmas was approaching, it occurred to me that we had the perfect setup for a nativity scene. I wondered if David could make a manger of some sort and I could make some little costumes, and together we could put together a scene for a photograph. David is an amateur photographer, so when I mentioned my thoughts to him he liked the idea and suggested that if the picture turned out as we hoped it would, we could include it in our Christmas cards that year.

It wasn't long before the manger had been nailed together out of some rough boards, the costumes were sewn, and the children assembled for the much-anticipated "Kodak moment." Charlotte, seven, made a lovely little Mary; Sarah, five, was a cute, curly-headed angel; Jason, almost three, was an adorable shepherd; and Daniel, five months, was, of course, the baby. The older three were costumed, patiently waiting and observing as I attempted to wrap their squalling brother in swaddling clothes (how *did* Mary do that?). Then Charlotte could no longer keep her maternal-like concerns to herself. She shook her scarfed head and with a troubled expression said, more to herself than to me, "I wouldn't put *my* baby in that dirty old manger."

My struggle against Daniel's flailing arms and legs immediately stopped. Kneeling on the floor beside Daniel, I reached over and drew Charlotte close to me and looked into her concerned little face. At first I could say nothing. The words my little girl had spoken smote me as no telling or retelling of the Christmas story has before or since. "Charlotte," I said to her softly when I had regained control of my emotions, "first of all, that manger isn't dirty. The straw is fresh and clean and Daniel is going to be wrapped up in cloth with a blanket underneath him. But, Honey, don't you see? Even if that weren't so, Daniel will only be in that manger for a few minutes. At home he has the beautiful cradle that Daddy made for him *and* a nice, comfortable crib. A dirty old manger is *all* that Jesus had. He was the Creator of the universe, and His only bed was a feeding trough in a filthy stable."

I was choking back tears then, just as I am now in relating it to you. I gave Charlotte a tight squeeze and resumed preparation for our family photo shoot. Daniel finally submitted to having his chubby legs swaddled. I gave in and left his arms free. The older children cooperated beautifully, and as quickly as you can say "Cheese!" we had our 1985 Christmas card picture.

As you might guess, we left the scene of that photography session with a whole lot more than a photograph. We carried away with us a profoundly deeper understanding of heaven's awesome sacrifice on that first Christmas morning. And though we didn't know it at the time, we also took with us the beginning of a family tradition. For 13 consecutive years, David has made props and developed innovative lighting techniques, I have designed scores of costumes, and the children have posed, through all manner of weather conditions and strange situations, for Christmas card pictures. The memories we have of putting together those annual photographs would fill another book. And that is, after all, what traditions do best—they help us to remember.

Don't be deceived into thinking that all traditions must be major productions. That is not the case. Traditions can be as simple as something you always say at a particular time or occasion. "Nite, nite, I love you," has always been our bedtime sign-off, and no one at our house goes to bed without saying it.

As soon as our children were old enough to roam farther than the end of our sidewalk, I started regularly saying to them, "Bye. I love you. Have fun. Be careful. Remember who you are." When they got older they began to tease me about it, but I could tell it was something that they really didn't mind. In fact, I sensed their enjoyment of it. This was confirmed later when I learned that Sarah, who spent two months working with missionaries in Australia, said the exact same thing to the people there in Brisbane as they left the house where she was staying.

By the time she left Australia, some of those people were saying it to their loved ones! So if you're ever Down Under and hear an Aussie shouting "my" goodbye to a departing child, you'll know that it originated in the humble house of a loving family in a little country town in Virginia. Who would have ever imagined it?

Now be encouraged, my Child. You undoubtedly have dozens of ideas of your own for leading your wonderfully unique family into a future of fondly cherished memories, and every new day will spawn even more. But before you run off to set those ideas into motion, permit me to remind you that the best things in life are free, and the next-best things in life are inexpensive. Your children will emerge into adulthood with a plethora of pleasant memories if you spend time rather than money on them. A fortune spent does not good memories make.

Now run along to your family and let the good times roll. Bye. I love you. Have fun. Be careful. Remember who you are!

> Ah, then how sweetly closed those crowded days!
> The minutes parting one by one like rays,
> That fade upon a summer's eve.
> But O, what charm or magic numbers
> Can give me back the gentle slumbers
> Those weary, happy days did leave?
> When by my bed I saw my mother kneel,
> And with her blessing took her nightly kiss;
> Whatever Time destroys, he cannot this; –
> E'en now that nameless kiss I feel.
> — Washington Allston

Homes are for mothers as nests are for birds.
—Arthur B. Laughlin

13

Oh, Yes
You Can!

For much of this book I've been talking to you about the in-
tangibles of making a house a home: making sure your foundation is the solid Rock; building relationships through changed
attitudes; leaving the past behind; taking responsibility for your
own behavior; and laying down your life for the good of your
husband and children. Those are, by far, the most important
(and difficult) issues for you to consider as you strive to create
a heavenly home for yourself and your family. The most mag-
nificently decorated house in the world will never make up for
failure in those areas. You already understand that, I know, and
are cooperating with God as He transforms you and leads you
to certain victory. I'm cheering you on, dear Child; my prayers
follow you.

With the more difficult tasks and realizations already under-
way, we can now enjoy the pleasure of talking about some of the
tangibles of creating an extraordinary home. This is the fun
part. In fact, compared with the other work we've been discussing, this is recreation. While building relationships is the
most essential aspect of making a house a home, preparing a
"place" for your family is important too. God plainly thinks so,
for all that Jesus said and did was a reflection of the Father to
us. Jesus carried out every conceivable (and inconceivable) bit
of work necessary to bring you into proper relationship with

Himself, even to the laying down of His life for you. He also made this spectacular promise: "There are many rooms in my Father's House. If there were not, should I have told you that I am going away to prepare a place for you? It is true that I am going away to prepare a place for you, but it is just as true that I am coming again to welcome you into my own home so that you may be where I am" (John 14:2-3, Phillips). Think of it! Jesus is preparing a place for you just as you are setting about to prepare a place for your loved ones. It makes your job as a wife and mother sound like a high and holy calling, doesn't it? And so it is.

Being called to "prepare a place," as wonderful as it may sound, is a stumbling block to some women because they are sure they lack the ability to do it well. "You have such a knack about decorating," a discouraged friend said to me one afternoon. "I would *love* for my house to look like this, but I'm just not artistic or talented the way you are."

I've heard similar stories from many others, and I've given a great deal of thought to this complaint. Of course not everyone shares the same abilities and talents, but everyone does have some ability. To say otherwise is the same as saying, "God left me out. He didn't give me any talents. I simply cannot do things the way other people can. The living, loving God of heaven overlooked me and made me a special case."

Could anyone possibly believe that God called her to home-making but didn't equip her for the task? No, I don't think so either.

But you have had such feelings at times, haven't you? I wish I could place my arm around you and assure you that first, those feelings are deceptive, and second, you aren't alone in having them. As a matter of fact, women at least as far back as 1871 suffered from the ill-conceived notion that they simply weren't cut out for their homemaking duties. In her book *Common Sense in the Household*, published in that year, Marion Harland counsels this way:

You have seen the time—nay, many times since you have assumed your present position [of homemaker] when you would have exchanged your knowledge of ancient and modern languages, belles-lettres, music, and natural science, for the skill of a competent kitchen-maid. The "learning how" is such hard work! Labor, too, uncheered by encouraging words from mature housewives, unsoftened by sympathy even from your husband or your father or brother, or whoever may be the "one" to whom you "make home lovely." It may be that, in utter discouragement, you have made up your mind that you have "no talent for these things."

I have before me now the picture of a wife, the mother of four children, who many years ago sickened me for all time with that phrase. In a slatternly morning gown at four in the afternoon, leaning back in the laziest and most ragged of rocking chairs, dust on the carpet, on the open piano, the mantel, the mirrors, even on her own hair, she rubbed the soft palms of one hand with the grimy fingers of the other, and with a sickly-sweet smile whined out–"Now, I am one of the kind who have no talent for such things! The kitchen and housework and sewing are absolutely hateful to me, utterly uncongenial to my turn of mind. The height of my earthly ambition is to have nothing to do but to paint on velvet all day!"

. . . If you have not what our Yankee grandmothers termed a "faculty" for housewifery—yet are obliged, as is the case with an immense majority of American women, to conduct the affairs of a household, bills of fare included—there is the more reason for earnest application to your profession. If the natural taste be dull, lay to it more strength of will—resolution born of a just sense of the importance of the knowledge and dexterity you would acquire. Do not scoff at the word "profession." Call not that common and unclean which Providence has designated as your life-work.[1]

And that is exactly what I would say to you, Daughter. You must not focus on the difficulty of the task nor on your perceived deficiencies. The wrong focus is what cripples you. You wouldn't believe how many things I've done that I "can't" do. John Stuart Mill, a 19th-century British philosopher, said, "The pupil who is never required to do what he cannot do, never does what he can do." And that leads me to another very important point.

In my house, there's a phrase that has been relegated to outer darkness, never to be spoken—even whispered—by a soul. This ban is strictly enforced. Infractions are never tolerated. The unlawful words are "I can't."

So as I give you suggestions, a few how-tos and loads of encouragement in "making home lovely," you must not even think of using those nasty, whiny, immobilizing words. "I can't" is a self-fulfilling prophesy; there are no possibilities in it. A brick wall has more pliability than does a person who always complains, "I can't." My declaration to you is a hearty, "Oh, yes you can!"

But will you try? That is up to you, Child. Only you.

Now that we understand each other well, I'm eager to share with you a few of the techniques and ideas I have acquired over the years. Most of these I've learned by observing other people in their homes and by doing a little research in books and magazines. The library is full of resources that will help you in every conceivable area of home decorating. Do some investigating to discover what type of furnishings and decorating appeal to you most. Consider carefully the colors with which you want to live. What does your husband like? Is he strongly opinionated about how your home should look, or does he leave that decision entirely up to you? (My husband is of the latter mentality, caring only about how much it will *cost*.) What will work well with your style of house and with your lifestyle? What can you afford? What will you be able to afford in the future?

When I told my husband what I would be writing about in this chapter, he said to me, "Tell them first of all to get out their checkbooks." We both laughed, thinking of our eight years in our 98-year-old money pit. When we first drove into the gravel driveway of this old, rundown farmhouse, we had no idea what we were getting ourselves into financially. In fact, when we signed the contract on this place we thought we were setting ourselves up for financial freedom. After all, couldn't we do nearly all of the needed work on the house ourselves? As fiscally conservative and careful as David is, I was confident that no detail had escaped his consideration as he and I purchased our "inexpensive" house in the country.

The truth is, some situations are impossible to anticipate, especially when fixing up an old building. The owning of "This Old House" is definitely not for the fainthearted.

Come to think of it, owning *any* house is a bold financial adventure, but it can be a wise one as well. Many young couples pour a huge portion of their income into car payments, leaving them without the ability to save for the down payment on a house. Since cars depreciate in value, those families are actually making a vaporous investment of their income. By the time the cars are paid for they have very little value. Then they are sold or traded and the whole process begins again.

Generally speaking, the purchase of a home can be a sound investment. Unlike cars, real estate appreciates in value. Besides providing the necessary roof over your heads, a home can be a profitable financial venture. It is accompanied by responsibility, though.

Whether you're buying a house or renting a house or apartment from someone else, be it ever so humble, it's your home. Don't make the mistake of thinking, *I'm not going to do anything to this place because we aren't going to live here long. I'll wait until we have a nicer house (apartment, condo, fill in the blank), and then I'll care about fixing it up.* Please don't live your life in the future. Tomorrow is not promised. Today is given. Begin now, no matter where you are. "Life wastes itself while we are preparing to live," said the sagacious Ralph Waldo Emerson.

Don't be discouraged by a lack of funds either. Our family has always had to operate within that restriction. There are a multitude of things you can do to beautify your home that cost little or nothing. If the most you can do is place some handpicked wild flowers in an empty vanilla extract bottle on your dining table, then do it. Every effort you make is worthwhile. God sees and will remember even the feeblest labor of love.

Before going any further, permit me to tell you what I have always impressed upon my children: the most important rule of homemaking is to begin with *clean and neat*. A dirty house cannot be beautiful. We talked extensively about this earlier, so I won't nag you about it anymore. Besides, I wouldn't want you to become as preoccupied with the subject as was the poor housewife who, before dying in 1967, had inscribed on her tombstone, "Excuse my dust."[2]

Next, I would advise you to *never* pay full price for anything for your home. Everything from sheets to sofas is on sale somewhere every day. Be alert and patient. Buying necessities on sale stretches your budget and enables you to do more with the amount God provides. This is part of the meaning of Proverbs 31:11-12: "Her husband has full confidence in her and lacks nothing of value. She brings him good, not harm, all the days of her life." A virtuous woman (that phrase speaks of excellence, moral worth, ability and mobility, not just marital fidelity) is, among many other things, frugal with money.

Above all else, do everything with a view toward making your home a witness for Christ. Our homes say more than we like to think about the One in whom "we live and move and have our being" (Acts 17:28). When a person approaches your home and steps in the front door, what impression will she receive about your lifestyle, your values, your focus? Don't kid yourself into thinking that no impression is being made. It certainly is! Upon entering your home, an individual is struck by a combination of auditory, visual and olfactory stimuli that effect an immediate impression, whether positive or negative. If God has blessed you with a roof over your head, however modest, why not thank Him by making your home a sacrifice, a sweet savor unto Him? I'll give you a few ideas on how this may be accomplished. Ask God for some ideas too. He'll be delighted to help you turn your home into a lighthouse for Him.

What should we consider first, then, in your quest for a beautifully appointed home? Style is a good place to begin. What's yours? Have you ever thought about it? Do you like modern? Country? Traditional? Victorian? An eclectic mix? Think about houses you've visited or seen in magazines. What appeals to you? It may seem silly for me to ask these questions, but I've met many women who've never pinned down their style preferences, so they just float along without focus in their decorating. You're going to accumulate furnishings and accessories whether or not you give it much thought. If you just roll along like a tumbleweed, you probably won't be satisfied with the end result. Once you've decided the overall style(s) with which you'd like to live, assess what you already have that fits, or can be made to fit, that style. Build from there, and be prepared for years of working on the "finished product." Most of the fun in putting a home together is the *process*. Relax and learn patience. Home wasn't built in a day.

Remember also that as you grow and mature, your tastes may drastically change. As a newlywed I liked things that I now think were hideous. Our evolving style is part of the process too. Don't hold too tightly to anything. Things are just that—*things*. Someday they'll all burn, so don't take yourself or any of this decorating business too seriously.

After style, the next most important consideration is color. Color sets the mood of every room: bold and bright, soft and subdued, light and airy, dark and dramatic. Decide what you like, what suits your family and fits your style, and go with it. Ignore trends. Who cares what's in style for houses this year? Next year it will be something different. Are you willing to redecorate every year or two? Of course not. So simply follow your heart where color is concerned, and I'll wager you'll never end up with avocado appliances or neon shag carpeting. (Why *did* people do that?)

I admit that I have known a few individuals who have no concept of color coordinating whatsoever. I even know one woman who has to ask her husband if her clothes match! In a case like that I wouldn't recommend that you make major decisions regarding colors for the house alone. Your husband should be involved in these decisions in any case, but a friend with an eye for color can be helpful if your husband is disinterested or lacks confidence in his own ability. It may be helpful as well to peruse the pages of some of the home decorating magazines on the market (such as *Traditional Home, Country Living, Country Home, Colonial Homes* and *Southern Living*). You're sure to find something that appeals to you there. Cut out pictures and take them to your local paint store. The people who mix the paint for you can help you achieve the same look without the guesswork. Often paint stores sell wallpaper and coordinating fabrics as well, and have knowledgeable employees who can help you with your color-related decisions. If you need help, don't hesitate to ask for it.

While we're on the subject of color, let me put in a good word for plain old paint. Nothing can do more to transform a room than a fresh coat of it. There are a few things to know before running headlong into a major painting project. No one is *born* knowing this stuff. David and I learned it through 22 years of trial and error—lots of error. Here are a few discoveries we've made:

1. Never buy the cheapest paint available; you'll get poor coverage and it won't wash well. You certainly don't have to buy the most expensive brand on the market either. Something in the middle range should be adequate. If you would rather buy the higher-priced paint, at least wait until it's on sale. Whatever paint you buy, make sure it claims to be scrubbable, especially if you have or plan to have children. Peanut butter fingerprints do not wash off all painted surfaces equally. Be reasonably sure that your paint can stand up to family-made messes.

2. Never paint bare wood surfaces without first priming them. You'll be wasting your time and your money if you do.

3. Everything except paint is darker when wet and dries lighter. Paint is lighter when wet and dries darker. If you roll a few strokes of paint on the wall and your immediate impression is that the shade is darker than you wanted, stop painting! It

will be even darker when dry. If you keep going you will either have to live with a color you don't like, or you'll end up re-painting the entire room.

4. If you decide to lighten the color of paint (whether it be a very small amount or a gallon or more), don't make the mistake we once made. Add your too-dark paint to the lighter paint in-stead of the other way around. If you try to lighten the shade of a gallon of paint by adding the light paint to the dark, you may wind up with numerous gallons before you achieve the shade you desire. Try finding a use for nine gallons of pastel pink paint! Your baby girl will be away in college before you use even the fifth can. (Unfortunately, I speak from experience.)

5. Latex paint (water-based) must never be applied on top of oil-based or alkyd paint. It won't stick—period. If you live in a house that was built in the 1950s or before, chances are that the paint first used in your house was oil-based. If you're not sure, take a chip of the old paint to a paint dealer and he'll probably be able to tell you. If the paint is oil-based, either remove it and then repaint with latex, or go ahead and use oil-based paint.

6. One coat of even the highest-quality paint doesn't do an adequate job. Make the effort of applying two coats of paint (or more if necessary, as would be the case if you are applying a light over a darker color). It doesn't take that much longer, and you'll see the results of your labor if you go the extra mile.

Before leaving the subject of paint, I want to encourage you that painting a room or an entire house of rooms can seem a daunting task if you've never done it before. But it really isn't hard at all. Ask your paint dealer for his advice on types of paint, the suitable equipment and appropriate painting meth-ods for your job. He'll be able to tell you everything you should know before you begin.

Oh, one more thing. Wear old clothes. You *will* get paint on yourself. (Again, I speak from experience.)

Once you've stroked some paint on a few walls, you may be ready for something a bit more challenging, especially if you have some rather mundane rooms you'd like to liven up. Look into some alternative painting techniques such as sponging, ragging, strippling and combing. Many stores that sell paint also sell supplies and have informative literature for these methods. All four methods (and there are many others) lend a subtle textured look to your walls that achieves a unique "specialness" at little cost. If your paint store does not have information about creative painting techniques, try the library. You're sure to find some answers and illustrations there.

Don't be afraid to veer away from convention with paint colors. Ceilings don't *have* to be white. Eggshell is not the only acceptable color for walls. You have personality all your own. Lend some of it to your house. Walls are the background for all of your other decorating. Make them interesting and inviting.

An alternative to painted walls is, of course, wallpaper. While papering is more expensive than painting (sometimes much more so), it opens up multitudes of possibilities: papering the walls halfway up; using borders; papering some walls and painting others; and using two or more coordinating papers. There are so many types and styles of wallpaper that there are entire stores devoted to the sale of them. Most of these stores will permit you to check out a few sample books so you can take them home and compare the samples against your carpet and upholstery and curtain fabrics before making a decision. Wallpaper can be a major purchase, so take care in choosing the right one.

Many people I know are afraid to attempt the application of wallpaper themselves. What a shame. It isn't all that difficult and becomes twice as costly when you have to pay someone to do it for you. If you've never done any papering, see if you can catch an opportunity to watch someone else do part of a room. When you decide to go ahead and try it, perhaps start with a small room, or a room where only half the wall is to be papered, such as where walls are divided by chair railing. All you'll need for the job (besides the paper) are scissors; single-edge razor blades; a plumb line; wallpaper paste and paint brush, if the paper comes unpasted; a large container of water (we use a full-sized cooler), if the paper comes prepasted; a large sponge; a stepladder; and some patience.

It may seem a little awkward at first, but once you get the hang of it (sorry, I couldn't help myself) you'll wonder why anyone would pay someone else to do it for her. After you paper a few rooms you may find that your friends are willing to pay you for the service. David has earned some extra money for us several times by wallpapering. Once, he papered his sister's bathroom in exchange for a microwave oven. She had one she wasn't using and we didn't have one yet, so that was a great deal for her and for us. Learning new skills opens up all kinds of possibilities. That's how many cottage industries are born.

If you're still not convinced that you are capable of wallpapering, perhaps you could trade a skill you have (baking, babysitting, typing) in exchange for the wallpapering skills of a friend. It's a great way to do business.

Perhaps you like the look of wallpaper but are still hesitant to go to the work and expense. I recommend stenciling as a remarkably easy, economical alternative. (I feel as if I can speak on this subject with some authority since I ran my own stenciling business for more than ten years.) Stenciling is not the least bit messy and, contrary to common belief, the stencil "artist" need not be artistic at all. As with any other new pursuit, you'll need practice and a little patience to achieve success. You can't expect perfection the first time you try anything. Never give up; try again. Some people fear failure so much that they never try anything new. If you have that attitude, ask yourself this question: "What is the worst possible thing that can happen if I try this and find I'm not good at it?" You'll be no worse off than you are now, will you? But what might happen if you try something new and discover that you actually have a propensity for it? The possibilities are endless. Don't bar the door to them.

The first time I saw stenciling was in a magazine. I was immediately drawn to it as a decorative enhancement. After I read a short history of stenciling and looked into how it is done, I decided to give it a try. My first project was our living room walls, and I was astounded at how easily and quickly the room was transformed. It took about three hours, start to finish, but we were still enjoying the compliments years later when we moved from that home. Does that spark your interest a bit?

Speaking of "spark," did you know that the word *stencil* derives from *estenciler* (Old French), meaning "to adorn brightly," and from *estencile*, meaning "spark"? In the 13th-century there was a vogue for dark-painted walls with sparkling gold stars. To stencil meant "to scatter with stars."[3]

After printed wallpaper became available in the 17th century, stenciling remained popular as a poor man's decoration, especially in America, where the already costly wallpapers had to be imported, adding to their cost. Stenciling was so popular in 17th-century America that some individuals made careers of the art. Itinerant stencil artists carried their paint and brushes wherever they went, offering their services in exchange for room and board. When one house was finished, the artist packed up brushes and personal items and moved on to another. Many stencil patterns from those colonial years have been reproduced and are still available today.

The most wonderful aspect of stenciling is that it is suitable to any type of decor, from southwestern to high Victorian to contemporary. In my farmhouse I've used simple colonial graphics, complicated Victorian florals and some original designs to fit the theme of a particular room. Most of the time I use a stencil pattern as a border around the upper edge of walls. I also have done an overall pattern on walls similar to wallpaper. Anything goes with stenciling. It's an ancient art that adapts to every age and taste.

Lean a little closer and I'll tell you the deep, dark secret of those itinerant stencilers: anybody, and I mean *anybody*, can stencil. The results can be so stunning that you would think the procedure must be complicated, requiring a great deal of skill or talent. That is simply not the case. Of course, if everyone knew that, no one would pay someone else to do it, so the "artists" kept their mouths shout. Even stencilers have to eat, I suppose.

As an aside, I must tell you that the only problem
enced with stenciling is the fact that most of it mus
while perched on a ladder. From the time I was a sm........ ....,
was so terrified of heights that I couldn't make it more than two
steps up a ladder, and even then I would be shaking and hug-
ging the ladder as if it and I were suspended a hundred feet in
the air. Never could I have imagined myself standing on the top
step of a ladder with both hands free for stenciling around the
upper edge of 12-foot walls; but I've done it dozens of times.
You see, it was something I wanted *badly* to do. That gave me
the firmness of purpose to overcome an almost-crippling fear,
while at the same time mastering an art that has enhanced our
home and the homes of many others. It also enabled me to sup-
plement our family's income while doing something I enjoyed
immensely. Determination exerts more power than does ability.

Paints, stencil brushes and stencils are available at most craft
and many department stores. Home decorating magazines usually have advertisements for stenciling catalogs in the back.
These catalogs offer a much wider selection of stencils than
you'll find in stores. Many stencils come with very clear instructions, but if not, the local library and bookstore provide
plenty of resources for the how-tos of stenciling.

Not only walls, but fabric, furniture, floors, stationery—almost anything—can be stenciled. Because of this, stencils are
available in many different sizes. Just remember that a one-inch
stencil design might be perfect at the top of your stationery but
will disappear on your wall. A wall border needs to be more
substantial in size. If you stencil around the upper edge of your
walls, the work will be viewed from a distance and thus look
smaller. In temporal as well as spiritual things, perspective is
everything.

I also have learned that I can make my walls talk. Not that
they have ever spoken a word, mind you. But they do testify of
family love and of devotion and of Christ. How? I can't wait to
tell you.

Walls are simply the canvas and frame for the picture you wish to paint. The objects displayed on your walls speak of you: what is important to you, what appeals to you, what you believe. What are your walls saying to people about your life and your faith?

Almost everyone would desire to live with beautiful displays of artwork and design, yet few of us can afford such luxury— or so it would seem. But what in the world is more beautiful to you than those you love? So what are all those photographs of your children, your parents and your grandparents doing stuffed in drawers and shoe boxes? Get them out, sort through them and hang your favorites on the wall. While frames can be extravagantly expensive, they don't have to be. All sorts of interesting frames can be purchased on sale or at discount stores at a very reasonable price. Buy one or two at a time until you have those wonderful photos framed.

Some photographs or portraits can stand alone, especially those larger than 8" x 10". Groupings can be stunning, though, and are very easy to put together. You might want to do a grouping for each of your children individually, or put photographs of all of your children together in one group. Photographs from a special vacation make a nice display, as well as pictures of ancestors and other relatives. Permit your walls to promote your family, to create a "hall of fame," if you will. Your family will recognize how important they are to you. Others will see it as well.

If you are thinking about having a family portrait done professionally, you might want to decide where the portrait will hang before you have the picture taken. If it will hang in your living room, which is painted and decorated in the palest of pastels, you don't want your family wearing their bright-red sweaters for the photo session. Plan ahead for a photograph that will be enhanced by its surroundings (and vice versa).

Sometimes renters face penalties for putting nail holes in the wall. If you are renting and would like to use family pictures without committing a punishable offense, why not display your photographs on tables, mantels, dressers and desks? The lovely faces of your loved ones speak of familial love wherever they're displayed.

Murals are another way to dress up walls, and you don't have to be Michelangelo to try drawing one. "But I can't even draw a straight line," you may protest. Who's suggesting that you draw a straight line? You can always use a measuring stick or a level for that. Don't knock your abilities before you've tried them. You may have talents galore cached behind that huge "I can't" of yours.

I never imagined that I could create paintings on our walls until I saw someone else do it. A good friend of ours, who also was not an artist, painted some charming pictures on the walls of his baby's bedroom. *What a cute idea,* I thought. *I wonder if I could do that.*

We were expecting our first child at the time, and I suppose it was the passion of pregnancy that pushed me quickly from wondering to working. In a few days I had picked out the pictures I wanted to copy onto our nursery walls and, armed with pencil, paint, a few artist's brushes and a whole bundle of willpower, I began my first murals.

In spite of my lack of even one art lesson and my total lack of experience in mixing and blending paints, the results were encouraging, so I was inspired to keep trying. Now, 20 years later, I have painted dozens of murals for our family, in many other homes and businesses and even in church nurseries. I'm so glad that 20 years ago I didn't say what would have been the perfectly logical thing: "I can't."

While painting wall murals has been fun and has lent a bit of charm and drama to our home, something much simpler has enabled us to make our home a testimony of our faith—Scripture verses and pithy sayings painted directly on the walls. God taught this idea to His people long ago: "These commandments that I give you today are to be upon your hearts. Impress them on your children. . . . Write them on the doorframes of your houses and on your gates" (Deut. 6:6-7, 9). Hanging up framed Scripture verses that have been written or calligraphied on paper is a fine way to make your faith known. There are many gorgeous examples of this for sale at Christian bookstores everywhere. But there really is something dramatic about Scripture written directly onto the wall. It isn't hard to do, either, even if you've never done anything like it before.

After choosing the verse you want to use and the spot where you want to put it, write it out on paper to get spacing even. Practice writing or printing the verse until you're satisfied with the way it looks. If your handwriting is positively illegible, you probably know someone with lovely handwriting who would be willing to put it on the wall for you. Perhaps you could barter with free babysitting or some other service in exchange for a little calligraphy. Preferably, though, you'll at least attempt to do it yourself. With a little practice, anyone's handwriting can improve.

It's very important to establish straight, level lines on the wall before you start writing. I always use a long level for this purpose, tracing the straight edge with a very faint pencil line. These lines are easily removed after the project is completed. (Never try to remove pencil marks from the wall with a pencil eraser. An eraser will leave shiny marks that are distracting and nearly impossible to remove. Instead, place your finger in the corner of a rag or cloth, dip it in warm water and then add a drop of liquid detergent and rub off the pencil lines or marks with ease.)

The verse should be penciled in next. Mistakes can be washed off and you can keep trying until it looks the way you want it. Then it's time to go over the penciled writing with an artist's brush and paint or a calligraphy pen. (If you decide to use a pen, make sure the ink is waterproof and fade proof.) The verses are a constant reminder to you of God and His wisdom, mercy and care. They are reminders to others as well—reminders that won't go unnoticed.

A few weeks ago our house was on our town's Christmas tour. It isn't a fabulous house, nor is it full of valuable antiques and such, so I'm always astonished and honored when we are asked to open our home. We relish the opportunity to see people enjoy the fruits of our labors, so we gladly consent to the weekend invasion. This time, more than a 1,000 people made their way through every room in our house, and the comments many of them made on their way out were heartening. "There's so much *love* in this house," several people commented. (Remember, they didn't observe much of our lives—only our house—before drawing such a conclusion.) "I love the way you have decorated with your children's pictures," others remarked. One women proclaimed loudly, "That was no house tour; that was a *home* tour!" Others leaned over to me and said quietly as if sharing a secret, "We *know* you're Christians," and, "Thank you for the quiet witness of your home."

Last week we received two letters from people in neighboring cities who attended the house tour. Excerpts from those letters follow:

> What a delightful home you have, and I just wanted to tell you by letter. It was such a joy to see all the work you have done on your home and also see all of your Christmas decorations. Thanks for opening your home for all to share. . . . My request is—could you possibly send me the Bible verses you have written on your walls in different rooms?

And,

> My family is so privileged to have walked through your home on the Smithfield Christmas tour. What a blessing that your very walls spoke out TRUTH to the throngs you opened your doors to in hospitality on that weekend.

God said His Word will not return to Him empty "but will accomplish what I desire and achieve the purpose for which I sent it" (Isa. 55:11). Whether proclaimed from a pulpit or etched upon your walls, His Word does its work. And you, my Child, can be a participant in that labor of love. To God be the glory!

One more suggestion for filling up wall space is the use of quilts. Yes, I know quilts are for use on the bed, but they are also works of art and can be quite stunning if displayed on a wall. They help absorb sound, too, which can be a real plus in a house full of children. Beauty and soundproofing in one fell swoop!

That's about all I can think of that you might want to do to your walls. You'll probably come up with more ideas as you go along. Remember, it's *your* home, so let it reflect *your* family's personality. That's what makes every home unique. Cloned homes are not what we're after. Emulation can be profitable and inspiring, but only to the degree that it helps you to become all that God meant *you* to be.

Floors are an aspect of decorating that cannot be ignored, but from a financial point of view it would be good if they could. Floors and floor coverings are expensive. Whether you're looking at wall-to-wall carpeting, rugs, vinyl, tile, wood or wood veneer, it's going to cost a small fortune to replace what you already have. If the floor you're living with now is unbearable, start saving. Don't buy on credit. It will be expensive enough without paying interest.

You probably already have a good idea of the type of floor covering you want. Wall-to-wall carpeting is comfortable, comes in an extravagant selection of colors and a wide range of prices. Many people resist buying lighter shades of carpeting because it would seem to dirty more easily. Why not practice removing your shoes at the door? Then you may choose any shade of carpet you like without having to worry about tracking in dirt. Your guests, of course, may wear their shoes in, because it's the everyday family wear and tear, not the occasional visitor, that ruins carpet.

If you decide to go with carpet, purchase the best padding available to go underneath it. The life of the carpet is in the padding.

Deciding on a color of carpeting can be difficult. A room may be adorned with three or more complementary colors, but one color should dominate. Since carpeting covers such a large area of a room, it should be either neutral or the dominant color of that room. Having two or three colors vying for eminence in one room makes the room buzz and lack focus. You might want to choose one color for your carpet and, say, your window valances, and then use other colors as accents.

Vinyl floors offer another horde of options. Vinyl varies greatly in quality and durability. The expensive products have color all the way through the flooring; the more affordable vinyls have a layer of color or pattern only on top. Shooting for the mid-price range is usually a good idea, if possible. If the floor is in a heavy traffic area you'll want to avoid the vinyls with a superficial finish. They simply will not hold up. Save a while longer and buy something that will give you better service.

The wood floors in our farmhouse are painted. The best we can tell, they were painted from the time the house was built. We even uncovered an original design of colorful, 14-inch squares and diamonds that had been painted on our foyer floor. Since the floors were not in very good shape and had to be partially replaced, we decided to keep them painted instead of trying to remove all the paint and refinishing them. The results were very pleasing. In our foyer, the dominant color is cream with peach and black accents, so we painted the floor cream (with floor and deck enamel), and I stenciled a Victorian pattern around the perimeter of the room in black. Everyone raves about it, and it was much less expensive than carpeting or any other floor covering would have been.

Whatever type of flooring or floor covering you choose, remember that it is part of the general scene against which the rest of your decorating is viewed. Don't make snap decisions. Consider all of your options carefully; you'll probably have to live with your choice for a long time.

Window coverings offer an even larger list of options. Anything and everything and nothing goes for windows. If you have a beautiful view and no need for privacy, putting nothing on your windows is a very real option. If privacy is your main concern, blinds or shades are probably the way to go. Even if you use those options you may want to "dress up" your window with an over-treatment of curtains, draperies, valances or swags. If you know how to sew, this is an area where you can shine and save money at the same time. Plain curtains with a rod pocket and straight hem are about the simplest sewing project there could be. Even those who claim to be unable to sew a stitch should at least try their hand at straight curtains.

Simple unlined swags and valances are easy, too, if you work up to them. Look for patterns that say "EASY" or "SIMPLE" on them. True to their name, these usually have easy-to-understand instructions with them. Whatever window treatment you choose, you can usually make it for less than half of what you will pay for ready-made curtains.

Another idea is to use items for window dressing that were originally meant for other purposes. For example, in my kitchen I have one oval window that needs no covering, and one tall, narrow window that I wanted to give a simple treatment. I ended up using an antique, oversized pillowcase top as a valance. This was easily mounted to the window frame with thumb tacks and makes for a cheerful look in its crisp, starched whiteness with red embroidery reading, "A glorious morning unto you."

I also have had success with using other uncustomary items as window accessories, such as tea towels, silk scarves and fringed, lacy, three-cornered shawls. (The latter make lovely drapes for fireplace mantels as well.) In our only full bathroom, which is decorated with sky, clouds, stars and angels, the only window in the room needed something simple and ethereal. I purchased six yards of inexpensive, sheer, white fabric, hemmed each end and ran the fabric through plaster brackets (purchased at a discount store), which were mounted on each side of the window frame top. I also ran a string of clear, tiny Christmas tree lights behind the entire length of fabric. The project cost very little and the effect is, well, heavenly.

I should interject here some advice that applies not only to window coverings but to every aspect of decorating: loosen up. Don't be afraid to innovate. Do something different or whimsical once in a while. "Pretty" isn't the only option. Some rooms are lost causes for "beautiful." Dramatic, charming and quaint are great to live with too. I have a little of all of those options in my house, and there isn't a room we don't enjoy.

Between my kitchen and dining room is a tiny space that isn't much more than a passageway between those two rooms. (Old houses are apt to contain some strange, nondescript cubicles of space. That is part of their charm.) The area is only four feet by five feet and has wainscoting and chair railing, as both the kitchen and dining room have. I had no idea what to do with that little space when we first bought the house. After some of the major repairs were completed and difficulties overcome in the house, I decided to give the tiny room some personality. Since I had a small collection of watermelon paraphernalia (seed packets, wooden watermelon replicas, photographs of our children eating watermelon, etc.), it occurred to me that this might be a good place to display it. Hence, my "watermelon room" was born.

First, I painted the walls a creamy white, then sponged on watermelon pink paint over that. After the paint dried I painted watermelon seeds all over the wall.

I painted the chair rail off-white, and the wainscoting at the bottom of the wall received a coat of dark green enamel, run through with the yellow-white squiggly lines characteristic of watermelon rind.

By the time the seed packets and pictures were hung and the watermelon collection displayed, the most ordinary space in the house became nearly everyone's favorite room. So, you see, where beauty isn't feasible, whimsy is always a possibility. Don't be so stiff in your decorating that you can't have any fun.

After telling you about my watermelon room it seems only natural that we should discuss the subject of collections. Collections can enhance any decor, especially when well displayed. I have a number of collections that I enjoy and use to set a theme for different rooms in our house. Most of my collections began without intent. I either purchased or was given an object and, later, was drawn to another and another until there it was—a collection. Some people set out to collect things, and that's fine too. However you may come by a collection, one thing is sure: the collection must be displayed to be enjoyed, and some methods of displaying are more effective than others.

When collected items are spread out over an entire house or several rooms, they do not make the visual impact that they would if placed closer together. For example, my kitchen (which is another one of those rooms where "pretty" wasn't an option) ended up with a bovine theme. The wallpaper is covered with cows, dairy farm signs adorn the walls, and my collection of cows graze peacefully everywhere from the refrigerator to the sink to the range to the Hoosier cabinets to the jelly cupboard. Everything is pulled together by the black and white squares on the floor.

Another collection that I enjoy is of old sleds and ice skates. Our family room is decorated with a winter theme and the sleds are strategically placed around the room. Some are hanging on the wall and one, my favorite, was made into our coffee table.

In the master bedroom I have an exquisite painting (a print of the painting, actually) of a flock of sheep standing in the snow at sunset as their shepherd dutifully approaches carrying their feed. Beneath the picture I have painted on the wall the words of one of my favorite Scripture verses, Isaiah 40:11a: "He tends his flock like a shepherd: he gathers the lambs in his arms and carries them close to his heart." On the fireplace mantel just under the verse is my collection of tiny sheep. It all comes together as a tranquil, bucolic scene of which I never tire, and which keeps me ever mindful of my faithful Shepherd's tender care of me.

My sons have a rather extensive seashell collection, which fits nicely into their nautically inspired bedroom. On one wall is a mural of an ocean with an inscription of Psalm 93:4: "Mightier than the thunder of the great waters, mightier than the breakers of the sea—the LORD on high is mighty." An old, wooden boat stands on end in one corner of the room. Shelves that David made go from side to side in the boat, and on them are displayed Jason's and Daniel's trophies, seashells and books. The sound of waves is the only missing element in this "seaside room."

Some people collect objects that were created for just that purpose—figurines and the like—and those collections can be extremely valuable. But *any* collection can have value to the collector, and that is what gives a collection its charm. I prefer having collections that mean something to me but have little or no monetary value. This preference was driven home powerfully by an experience I had about a year and a half ago.

A hurricane was headed for our area and I had a local speaking engagement. Hurricanes give a lot of advance warning, and since this one was more than 24 hours away, the women's group to whom I was to speak decided to go ahead with the meeting. When I arrived, several ladies were already present and there was a great deal of chatter about the impending storm. Some of the women had never ridden out a hurricane before and were full of questions for those of us who were natives. There was some apprehension in the group but no real anxieties, until a sweet-faced older woman entered the house. "Oh, I shouldn't have left home. I know I shouldn't," she moaned. She was visibly shaken, wringing her hands and pacing back and forth. I had no idea what was wrong, so I asked her to come sit beside me, which she did. "Calm down," I told her, "and tell me what's troubling you."

She took a deep breath, dabbed her forehead with a tissue and began. "I never should have come," she said. "I need to be at home helping my husband get ready for the storm."

"What is he doing?" I inquired.

"Oh," she lamented, "he's wrapping up all of my Precious Moments figurines so we can put them in the basement. I need to be there to help him. He'll never be able to finish by himself."

"Don't you have insurance?" I asked. "Couldn't you just replace them if they're broken?"

"Oh, no. You don't understand. Most of them are irreplaceable. They don't make them anymore." She stood up and began to wring her hands again. "I don't know what I would do if I lost those figurines. I just don't know what I would do."

That was the day I realized that I didn't want any *things* to be that important to me. That dear woman didn't own her collection; it owned her. What a miserable way to live.

If you have a collection, enjoy it and use it in a way that gives other people enjoyment too. Then if something happens to it, just release it and move on, realizing that everything temporal will pass away soon enough anyway. Never get too caught up in your possessions.

The only subject I'd still like to cover is that of making your home smell as good as it looks. Even as a young child, I recognized that every home has its own distinguishing smell. That knowledge fascinated me. I wondered why there would be such a vast difference in house scents. What made the difference from house to house?

It's still something of a mystery, but certain elements do make an obvious difference in the way a house smells: smoking in the house, indoor animals and cooking fish can leave unpleasant aromas in a home. Mustiness is another unsavory odor, and we've all visited houses that reek of moth balls. There are many disagreeable smells that can permeate a house, and any of us could discern them in someone else's home. The trouble is, we usually can't detect them in our own. We get desensitized to them. So it's a good idea to ask a close friend (whose honesty is dependable) what she smells upon entering your home.

Did you know that odors are more powerful memory makers than visual or auditory stimuli? That's why you can enter a kitchen where gingerbread cookies are baking and instantly be taken back to Grandma's house as a little child. We've all experienced olfactory time travel. So, we aren't finished with the subject of homemaking without a few words about creating a beautifully fragrant environment at home. Of course, the first thing to do is to eliminate sources of unpleasant odors, if possible. Clean up animal accidents as soon as they occur and keep your indoor pets clean and well-groomed. Try to correct moisture problems in the house, not only to improve the smell but to protect your property. Moisture is your house's mortal enemy. I'm sure I don't need to tell you all of the reasons why no one should be smoking in your house. Stale smoke odor is on the list, but it's probably at the very bottom. If at all possible, get cigarette smoke out of your house. Begin today.

Getting rid of offensive odors is only part of the solution; adding lovely scents is the other. There are myriad ways of doing this: scented candles, sachets, potpourri, room freshening sprays. You don't want to mix too many different fragrances in your home. No one wants to be overpowered, even by pleasant odors. Try different products and decide which one(s) suit you best, then stick with those.

If you're having company and you'd like your house to smell particularly yummy, try heating up some apple cider on the stove in an open pan. Apple juice works well, too, and costs less. Add some cinnamon and brown sugar, float orange slices studded with whole cloves on top, and simmer for a few hours. Everyone will enjoy the rich, spicy fragrance that will be wafting throughout your house. You can serve the concoction to your guests as well. This is an especially welcome treat in the fall and winter, but the scent is welcome year round.

Another little trick is to vacuum up a few pieces of potpourri or sachet beads while you're cleaning. Your vacuum cleaner will spread the lovely scent all over the house for you as you vacuum.

Of course, many types of flowers are very fragrant and, when brought into the house, can make a room smell like a spring garden. There are limits to the availability of flowers, but when you have them, use them. I can almost smell those gardenias you've so skillfully arranged in a vase on your kitchen table now. What a treat!

As you set about to transform your ordinary house into an extraordinary home, I hope a few of the ideas I've shared will be helpful to you, if only to stimulate your own cogitation and creativity. No matter how many other roles you play, if you are a wife and a mother, your primary profession is that of "preparing a place" for your dear ones. That preparation, while it certainly involves the actual physical labors of making and keeping a home, is far more intense in the unseen realm. It's all about relationships: your relationship to God, your relationship to your past ("forgetting what is behind"), and your relationships within your home.

When Jesus made His promise to go and "prepare a place for you," He understood fully all that must transpire before He could fulfill that covenant. First there would be death.

Before we can prepare a place for our loved ones, we also must die. The laying down of our lives—death to ambitions, death to our pasts, death to our rights, death to *ourselves*—is the paradoxical prerequisite to success. Only after we relinquish do we gain. Only after we lose do we find. Only after we die do we live.

I told you long ago that it wouldn't be easy, but, my dearest Child, be encouraged! It will soon be over. We labor and relinquish and lose yet but a little while. And even if no one understands how hard we labor, even if no one sees our sacrifice or pain, our toil on behalf of our loved ones does *not* go unnoticed; neither will it be in vain. The One who toiled on our behalf sees in secret. He is coming, and He brings His reward with Him! Listen again to His solemn, joyous vow:

> Do not let your hearts be troubled. Trust in God; trust also in me. In my Father's house are many rooms; if it were not so I would have told you. I am going there to prepare a place for you. And if I go and prepare a place for you, I will come back and take you to be with me that you also may be where I am. (John 14:1-3)

That is our blessed hope, Daughter. Not fancy houses. Not money or prestige or ease. But "the glorious appearing of our great God and Savior, Jesus Christ, who gave himself for us to redeem us from all wickedness and to purify for himself a people that are his very own, eager to do what is good" (Titus 2:13-14).

Continue to do all He shows you to do. Remember, it is always possible to do the will of God. Whenever you begin to doubt or fall into your old attitude of "I can't," do away with such thinking! Be assured of this—you can. Oh, yes you can!

> Oft-times the day seems long, our trials hard to bear,
> We're tempted to complain, to murmur and despair;
> But Christ will soon appear to catch His Bride away,
> All tears forever over in God's eternal day.
>
> It will be worth it all when we see Jesus,
> Life's trials will seem so small when we see Christ;
> One glimpse of His dear face all sorrow will erase,
> So bravely run the race till we see Christ.
>
> —Esther Kerr Rusthoi

Afterword

After reading my wife's book, you probably feel as if you know me. I think Glenda is much too extravagant in her praise of me, but I'm thankful for her love and esteem. I do not deny being a handyman, but I have never been a writer. I thought you might like a man's perspective of all this, though, so just for today I'll try my hand at writing.

The first thing I would want to say to you is something I have often said to our children: "Listen to your mother!" Proverbs 31:26 describes the virtuous wife as one who "speaks with wisdom, and faithful instruction is on her tongue." Glenda is that kind of wife, mother and spiritual mother. You will do well to hear and apply her teaching.

Many people have told Glenda and me that we have abilities that complement each other. I can certainly see how Glenda's abilities are needed to balance mine. If I had to make all the decisions in renovating the old house we live in, for example, every surface would probably be painted white, the walls would remain plain and undecorated, and nobody would ever ask to come inside just to see our house as they do now.

Our roles in establishing a home are likewise complementary. God gave me abilities and interests to affect our children's lives as their father: roughhousing and tossing them into the air when they were little; fixing their toys (and teaching them how to fix them); camping out in tents on cold, damp nights; teaching them math; fixing the old station wagon one more time so we could take a promised trip to the mountains; teaching them to drive.

Glenda, on the other hand, skillfully exercises her motherly touch. One night last week Charlotte called from college in Tennessee. Glenda answered the phone and started talking to her. I don't know all they talked about, but they had been talking for at least 15 minutes before I left to go to the hardware store (where else would a handyman be going?).When I returned 20 minutes later, they were still talking! I overheard some very good advice Glenda was giving to Charlotte: some was about boys, some about her studies, and some was just small talk that Charlotte probably needed to combat homesickness. If I had to fill that role I don't know what I would do. I might have been able to stay on the phone with her for 5 minutes (if she did most of the talking) before I ran out of things to say. I'm glad she calls home, and I'm glad her mother is here to answer the phone.

I'm also thankful that Glenda is always here to do the things she does that make our house a home for the six of us. It was a great comfort to know, when the children were small, that they were always with their mother and all was well.

I have always looked forward to arriving home at the end of the day, knowing the house would be in order, dinner would be in preparation and I would be greeted, after a hard day at work, with a smile and a kiss. One of my proudest memories was when I used to come home on a bus full of shipyard workers like myself and find my wife and two preschool daughters standing at the corner, dressed to the hilt waiting for me. Years later when I drove to work, my sons would wait for me at another corner hoping I would let them sit beside me and take the steering wheel as we crept down the narrow brick road to our house. These are just a few of my happy memories of the family and home God has given to me and of the wife who has faithfully orchestrated much of the happy goings on.

God has richly blessed me through His sovereign plan to make Glenda my wife. In Proverbs 31:5-31 God describes a noble or virtuous wife and begins by explaining how rare and valuable she is. Her faithfulness and hard work are described in great detail, as well as her kindness and business acumen. In verse 28 we are told that her children and her husband call her blessed and that her husband praises her.

So, in closing, that is what I would like to do: I thank you, Glenda, and give you praise, for being a virtuous wife to me, a loving mother to our children and a caring spiritual mother to other women. I can't say enough about the things you do to make our house a home. "Give her the reward she has earned, and let her works bring her praise at the city gate" (Prov. 31:31).

—*David Revell*
Smithfield, Virginia

The woman who creates and sustains a home, and under whose hands children grow up to be strong and pure men and women, is a creator second only to God.

—Helen Hunt Jackson

Notes

Chapter 2

[1] Hannah Whitall Smith, *The Christian's Secret of a Happy Life* (1870; reprinted Urichsville, Ohio: Barbour and Co., Inc., 1985), p. 214.

Chapter 3

[1] Frances de Sales, *Thy Will Be Done: Letters to Persons in the World* (1894; reprinted Manchester: Sophia Institute Press, 1995), p. 156.

[2] Theodore Monod, *Looking Unto Jesus* (Lincoln, Nebr.: Back to the Bible, 1991), pp. 23-24.

[3] Smith, p. 85.

[4] "Daring Thoughts: Selected Quotations From Deitrich Bonhoeffer's Writings," *Christian History,* Vol. X, No. 4 (1991), p. 12.

Chapter 4

[1] Oswald Chambers, *My Utmost for His Highest* (1935; reprinted Urichsville, Ohio: Barbour and Co., Inc., 1991), p. 91.

[2] Edwin Osgood Grover, ed., *The Book of Courage* (New York: The Algonquin Publishing Co., 1924), p. 24.

[3] Ibid., p. 29.

Chapter 5

[1] Ibid., p. 269.

[2] Ibid., p. 199.

[3] Much of what I have written about forgiveness and asking forgiveness was learned years ago at a Bill Gothard seminar (Institute of Basic Youth Conflicts).

Chapter 7

[1] Elisabeth Elliot, "The Two Selves," *Gateway To Joy.*

Chapter 8

[1] G. F. Maine, *A Book of Daily Readings* (London: Collins, n.d.), p. 29.

[2] Ibid., p. 46.

[3] Grover, p. 51.

[4] Maine, pp. 59-60.

Chapter 9

[1] Chambers, p. 218.

[2] Margaret J. Wise, ed., *Taste and See* (Chicago: Moody Press, 1972), p. 91.

[3] de Sales, p. 54.

[4] Elisabeth Elliot, "Courtesy," *Gateway To Joy*.

[5] Louise Bachelder, ed., *Little Things* (New York: Peter Pauper Press, Inc., 1992), p. 33.

[6] Elisabeth Elliot, "Let Me Be a Woman," *Gateway To Joy*.

[7] Bachelder, p. 12.

[8] Chambers, p. 188.

[9] Amy Carmichael, *If* (1938; reprinted Fort Washington, Pa.: Christian Literature Crusade, n.d.), p. 52.

[10] Bachelder, p. 22.

[11] Maine, p. 90.

Chapter 10

[1] Ibid., p. 14.

Chapter 11

[1] Chambers, p. 238.

[2] Elisabeth Elliot, *Let Me Be a Woman* (Wheaton, Ill.: Tyndale House, 1976), p. 95.

[3] Elisabeth Elliot, *Keep a Quiet Heart* (Ann Arbor, Mich.: Servant Publications, 1995), p. 20.

[4] Chambers, p. 260.

[5] Ibid., p. 270.

[6] Bachelder, p. 61.

Chapter 13

[1] Marion Harland, *Common Sense in the Household: A Manual of Practical Housewifery* (1871; reprinted Birmingham, Ala.: Oxmoor House, Inc., 1985), pp. 14-15.

[2] Nicola Gillies, *The Last Word: Tombstone Wit and Wisdom* (Oxford: Dove Tail Books, 1997), p. 60.

[3] Miranda Innes, *Miranda Innes' Country Home Book* (New York: Simon & Schuster, 1989), pp. 86, 89.